F. ROBERT PAULSEN became Dean of the College of Education at the University of Arizona in 1964, following similar deanship at the University of Connecticut 1961–64. For the most part, the thoughts in this book were drafted during these years.

Dr. Paulsen's well-rounded background as teacher, principal, and superintendent of schools preceded his serving as Professor of Educational Administration at the University of Utah from 1954 until 1961. Throughout his career he has received many honors and awards, including faculty study grants from both the Kellogg Foundation and the Carnegie Foundation. Dr. Paulsen serves on the boards of directors of several agencies in professional and commercial fields and is the author of a textbook on the administration of public education.

American Education

Challenges & Images

American Education

Challenges & Images

By F. ROBERT PAULSEN

THE UNIVERSITY OF ARIZONA PRESS
Tucson, Arizona

About the Author . . .

F. ROBERT PAULSEN became Dean of the College of Education at the University of Arizona in 1964, following similar deanship at the University of Connecticut 1961–64. His well-rounded background as teacher, principal, and superintendent of schools prefaced serving as Professor of Educational Administration at the University of Utah from 1954 until 1961. He has been the recipient of numerous honors and awards including faculty study grants from both the Kellogg Foundation and the Carnegie Foundation, serves on the boards of directors of several agencies in professional and commercial fields, and is the author of a textbook on the administration of public education.

THE UNIVERSITY OF ARIZONA PRESS

Copyright © 1967
The Arizona Board of Regents
Library of Congress
Catalog Card No. 66-28787
Manufactured in the U.S.A.

To the Reader

A MAJOR PURPOSE OF THIS PUBLICATION is to share some thoughts and ideas concerning the challenges and images of education today. For the most part, they were written when the author served as Dean of the School of Education at the University of Connecticut and Dean of the College of Education at the University of Arizona. Undoubtedly these ideas reflect a philosophy of life as well as of education. A basic tenet of the educational philosophy is summarized in the proposition that each person should be given the opportunity to develop his God-given faculties for the resolution of his problems and the achievement of the "good life," and that free public education is the best means we have to attain such an objective.

Each presentation was written for a specific purpose and thus may be read independently. Although the subjects treated are varied and diverse, there are several basic concepts and themes which appear throughout. Among these are considerations of the purposes of American education, the importance of self-realization and self-fulfillment as primary objectives of education, and the fact that various academic disciplines and professions all have contributions to make toward the understanding and development of the American educational system.

The responsibility of the educational profession to transmit the cultural heritage is self-evident and well accepted. There is an additional responsibility, however, for teachers and professors to help chart the direction of education. And there is a responsibility not to indoctrinate the young mind with what is perceived to be correct by those who instruct, but to teach respect for one's own search for truth. The search for truth is more meaningful if related to experience, and truth itself must be conceived as an ever widening horizon of fact and possibility.

In today's world, there is considerable need for more sentiment and more understanding of man as a human being. Such an understanding should be observed in the operation of our modern educational programs. And if an *idealist* is one who believes that we might continue to perfect ourselves through education, the author defers to the definition. It is doubtful, however, that these papers represent any classical philosophy of idealism.

[v]

One can still advocate a rigorous education based on scientific principles without forgetting that man is too complex to react as an automaton. One can believe that mental development and intellectual freedom must be foremost to the educator. We cannot ignore, however, the emotional component of the human being. One can aspire to the "good life" without being naïve by believing that everyone will find total happiness or that there will finally be established a utopia wherein mankind no longer need struggle to attain objectives and fulfill aspirations.

Inasmuch as many of these presentations were written originally as public and/or professional addresses, the support of general ideas seemed appropriate. Thus the author has quoted liberally from many sources. In the final presentation, documentation became a most important consideration. Apologies are made for any failure to give credit for ideas or sources of information which may have been overlooked or unobtainable.

The author is indebted to the editors of various professional journals for permission to include in this volume presentations which have appeared in previous publications. Among these journals are: *Educational Administration and Supervision; Journal of the American Physical Therapy Association; Journal of Educational Sociology; Social Work;* and the *Proceedings of the Utah Academy of Sciences, Arts and Letters.* The author is also indebted to the various authors and publishers cited for permission to use the quotations within this publication. Appropriate footnotes have been used throughout.

Appreciation is afforded to students and colleagues of the past years who have been provocative in inquiry and challenging in association. The encouragement of students and others to write and publish convictions and beliefs becomes a most meaningful source of motivation to the college professor.

F. Robert Paulsen

Contents

The capacity of our people to believe stubbornly and irrepressibly that this is a world worth saving, and that intelligence and energy and good will might save it, is one of the most endearing and bracing of American traits.

JOHN GARDNER

1. The Challenges to Education

THE REAL CHALLENGES to education in the twentieth century are considered but infrequently by the educators, community leaders, or national statesmen. Peripheral issues are discussed again and again, and many people appear to have a concern to change many aspects of various educational programs. Historically, however, most of the debates have indicated interest only with teaching techniques and methodologies. Even today there is considerable discussion about innovations in educational practice, but little is said about what kind of education is worth most. Seldom is there discussion and analysis of education in relationship to the maintenance and development of American civilization.[1] In effect, the society expends considerable physical and psychic energy in attempting to find solutions to immediate educational problems. In most instances, many basic issues of American education and society have not been understood or even considered by those persons who presume to lead other people toward individual self-fulfillment and societal destiny.

CRITICISMS OF AMERICAN EDUCATION

Many persons in the teaching profession become weary of the epithets hurled by critics who concern themselves only with insignificant issues framed with negative changes. Recently, for example, Admiral H. G. Rickover wrote a book entitled *American Education: A National Failure*.[2] In a nation which is proud of its social, technological, and cultural advancements, this title will hardly engender positive attitudes toward improving educational practices. If such criticism leads to anything, it leads to defensive countercharges by teachers and reinforcement of prejudices by critics. Such books may be profitable for authors and publishers, but they will do little to improve the American school

---

[1] *See:* Max Lerner, *America as a Civilization*, New York: Simon and Schuster, 1957; Robert Hendry Mathewson, *A Strategy for American Education*, New York: Harper and Brothers, 1957.

[2] New York: E. P. Dutton and Company, 1963.

system. Many critics should recognize the futility of effecting change in the human spirit by methods of ridicule and defilement.

Rather than debate and magnify many insignificant problems which are of little value to the teaching profession or the society, it is imperative to probe at greater depth the needs of human beings as individuals and of society in general. It is then necessary to relate the issues which emerge to our educational programs. If such an analysis is not made, mankind will surely drift aimlessly in the rapidly changing times of the current century.

Educational leadership today must not be equated solely to criticism of existing institutions and the professional performance of individuals. There is a justifiable place for criticism of any profession, field, program, or professional practice. If criticism is to be worthwhile, the critics must be at least as well informed as those whom they criticize. What is more, if critics are to be leaders, they must go one step beyond their communication of disagreement; they must draft the processes to be used in supplanting those things which seem in need of change. Present educational problems will hardly be solved by abolishing the American school system in favor of the English, Swiss, or even Russian patterns.

It is said that few situations are without some historical precedent, but educational leaders of today do face issues without parallel. Children and adults of the twentieth century are confronted with problems never dreamed by their forefathers. The explosion of scientific knowledge and the accumulation of data concerning the earth and the universe are felt throughout every land.[3] Science has produced weapons which could destroy modern society. But science has also shown ways by which paradise could be established on earth. Avowed world revolutionists and dictators have indicated that ultimate objectives of their ideologies are to destroy and "bury" the Western world. Western civilization under the leadership of the United States continues to advance in a competitive manner the political ideology based on the importance of the individual. The society is more affluent, but the government is increasing controls which limit, in some degree, those things which have afforded affluence. These facts are apparent. The educator must deal with all of them.

The kinds of parent-teacher conferences, the adoption of new types of report cards, or the formulation of salary schedules for teachers

---

[3] Lyman Bryson, Editor, *An Outline of Man's Knowledge of the Modern World*, New York: McGraw-Hill Book Company, Inc., 1960.

and professors all wane in the background when one considers the really important educational problems which must be solved during the next few decades. Deteriorating school buildings, the shortage of qualified teachers, increased federal aid to education, and many new programs are some issues facing educators and parents. But those issues are small indeed when compared with more important challenges confronting American education today.

ISSUES OF THE CURRENT SOCIETY

Debates wax strong among various groups of men concerning the development of the private industrial ideology versus the need for new social and public enterprises.[4] This problem, along with those posed by urbanization and the counterproblems of suburban development, must be the concern of the educator.[5] The changing political scenes, both national and international, require sophistication of those persons who teach students about national goals and policy-making processes needed to achieve them.[6]

If broad issues of educational concern were listed, they would certainly include problems resulting from the population explosion, technological advancement, and the higher standards of living.[7] The secularization of our culture, supplanting a historically religious society, creates additional educational problems.[8] The teaching of ethical values and moral responsibility demands improved educational

[4]*See:* Adolph A. Berle, *The 20th Century Capitalist Revolution*, New York: Harcourt, Brace and Company, 1954; David Lilienthal, *Big Business: A New Era*, New York: Harper & Brothers, 1953.

[5]*See:* John C. Bollens, Editor, *Exploring the Metropolitan Community*, Berkeley: University of California Press, 1961; B. J. Chandler *et al.*, *Education in Urban Society*, New York: Dodd, Mead and Company, 1962; Michael Harrington, *The Other America*, New York: The MacMillan Co., 1962.

[6]*See:* The American Assembly, *Report of the President's Commission on National Goals*, *Goals for America*, New York: Prentice-Hall, Inc., 1960; Michael Curtis, Editor, *The Nature of Politics*, New York: Avon Book Division, The Hearst Corporation, 1962; Seymour M. Lipset, *Political Man*, New York: Doubleday and Company, 1960; W. W. Rostow, *The United States in the World Arena*, New York: Harper & Brothers, 1960.

[7]*See:* Leonard Freedman and Cornelius P. Cotter, Editors, *Issues of the Sixties*, Belmont, California: Wadsworth Publishing Co., 1963; The American Assembly, *Automation and Technological Change*, Englewood Cliffs, New Jersey: Prentice-Hall, Inc., 1961.

[8]*See:* Martin E. Marty, *The New Shape of American Religion*, New York: Harper & Brothers, 1959.

endeavor.[9] Even though communism has been contained at the present time, and there is a serious dispute between those two monolithic empires, China and Russia, the potential threat of communistic expansion remains. National survival will depend upon our ability to prevent this expansion.[10] Indeed, the prospect of improving the quality of the American way of life is an important educational challenge.[11]

Although issues such as these confront mankind today, there are even more important challenges to education.

Some people believe our basic educational problems involve the need for everyone to understand the technical knowledge of this scientific age with its emphasis on nuclear fusion and space rocketry. That everyone needs such understanding appears doubtful. The greatest educational challenges do not revolve around the sciences; rather they are related directly to helping man to become entirely human, to find himself, as it were, and through self-knowledge to attain a sensitivity for what is satisfying in life both for himself and his fellow men. Only in developing a renewed faith in his capacity to live, to love, and to grow, can man achieve the destiny for which his nature was designed.[12]

Many of the historical myths of man's relationship to the infinite may not be helpful in the modern age. Today we must become conscious of our strengths and limitations. If we are ever to live in peace and security, we must gain new insights into human strengths and weaknesses, human powers and inabilities. As Judson Herrick noted:

> We have won intellectual supremacy over the brutes, but that is not enough. We have not won control over our own brutish impulses for self-gratification at the expense of our neighbors. We have not learned that the voluntary renunciation of some personal and national advantages is the only possible way to keep peace and win security and opportunity for cultural progress.[13]

Man has been called the time-binding animal. The mind of man, with abilities to symbolize, communicate, and remember, character-

---

[9]*See:* Donald N. Barrett, Editor, *Values in America*, Notre Dame: University of Notre Dame Press, 1961; Abraham H. Maslow, Editor, *New Knowledge in Human Values*, New York: Harper & Brothers, 1959.

[10]*See:* N. S. Khruschev, *The Revolutionary Working Class and Communist Movement*, Moscow: Foreign Languages Publishing House, 1963.

[11]*See:* John W. Gardner, *Excellence*, New York: Harper & Brothers, 1961.

[12]*See:* C. G. Jung, *Memories, Dreams, Reflections*, recorded and edited by Aniela Jaffe, New York: Pantheon Books, 1963.

[13]*The Evolution of Human Nature*, New York: Harper & Brothers, 1956, p. 221.

izes a unique creature. The cultivation of his reflective faculties elevates man out of the animal kingdom. The consciousness of self, the understanding of self, and the development of character afford the emergence of the whole man and the potential for ultimate communion with reality. It is to this end that mankind has directed purposive energies throughout the ages. The real challenges to American education are: (1) helping the individual understand his importance as a self-directed human being; (2) helping human beings learn how to communicate with one another; (3) helping people see the need for achieving national coherence; and (4) determining ways and means by which war and man's inhumanity to man might be abolished everywhere. Only through the accomplishment of these grand objectives will mankind show respect for himself and a common human destiny.[14]

THE BASIC ISSUES

The Self-Directed Human Being.   Over three decades ago, Oswald Spengler published his monumental study on *The Decline of the West*.[15] This philosopher of history had lost all faith in the productive capacity and free will of man. Spengler was convinced that Western culture had reached its zenith and was degenerating in the twentieth century like many great civilizations of the past.

For Spengler, the concept of "historical necessity" or "cultural determinism" replaced individual motivation and societal development as the mainsprings for the growth and innovations of culture. Essentially, he wrote on a deterministic theory of history which has been preached by prophets of doom since the days of antiquity.

> We have not the freedom to reach to this or to that, but the freedom to do the necessary or to do nothing. And a task that historical necessity has set will be accomplished with the individual or against him.[16]

In his contribution to a pessimistic and yet presumed noble philosophy of life, Spengler concluded his life's work by writing:

> Faced as we are with this destiny (ultimate decline and subjugation), there is only one world-outlook that is worthy of us ... better a short life, full of deeds and glory, than a long

---

[14]*See:* Henry Nelson Wieman, *Man's Ultimate Commitment*, Carbondale: Southern Illinois University Press, 1963.

[15] New York: Alfred A. Knopf Co., 1932.

[16]*Ibid.*, p. 507.

life, without content. Already the danger is so great, for every individual, every class, every people, that to cherish any illusion whatever is deplorable. Time does not suffer itself to be halted; there is no question of prudent retreat or wise renunciation. Only dreamers believe that there is a way out. *Optimism is cowardice.*

We are born into this time and must bravely follow the path to the destined end. There is no other way. Our duty is to hold on to the lost position, without hope, without rescue, like that Roman soldier whose bones were found in front of a door in Pompeii, who, during the eruption of Vesuvius, died at his post because they forgot to relieve him. That is greatness. That is what it means to be a thoroughbred. The honourable end is the one thing that cannot be taken from a man.[17]

At the same time that Spengler was expounding his cyclical theory of history and prophesying with "surety" the decline of the West, William P. Montague published a provocative essay calling for modern man to accept a new Promethean religion.[18] It is not necessary to agree with Montague to the extent that mankind should forsake his religions of the past and adopt a new mystical religion with a mythological component. It is interesting to note, however, the more positive contribution suggested in his development of a philosophy of life for those of us living in this age. Certainly we might understand the apparent *determinism* of our activities and yet contravene such determinism by developing those faculties of intellect and character which make us unique.

Perhaps all human beings act in accordance with their history. The past is present and operative in everyone. But the individual is still self-determined. The acts of the individual flow from his character and will. One can do what he wills in much of his life. He can will to do more than he does.

Montague wrote:

If the future were entirely and exclusively determined by the past, in each and every aspect of its form and matter, it would be so perfect a repetition of the past that it would be the past, and time itself would not go on. There would be no Passage. The present contributes something new and vital to the determination of the future. This is true of everything, everywhere, a little. But in human life, especially in moments of moral crisis, it is more than true.[19]

---

[17] *Man and Technics*, New York: Alfred A. Knopf Co., 1932, pp. 103–04.
[18] *Belief Unbound*, New Haven: Yale University Press, 1930.
[19] *Ibid.*, p. 53.

An essential goal of education will always be that of helping the individual find himself and be honest with and about himself and human nature. As Shakespeare, Freud, and other students of human behavior have noted, "To be completely honest with oneself is the very best effort a human being can make." This implies the prospects of attaining the "good" and healthy life — and beyond. We can agree with those who suggest that healthy people have satisfied the basic needs of security, belongingness, love, respect, and self-esteem to the point wherein they are motivated primarily by the desire to self-realization and the accomplishment of mission and destiny.[20] A superior perception of reality, considerable acceptance of oneself and of human beings generally, richness of emotional reaction, creativeness, and a more democratic character structure are traits indicative of the healthy person. These characteristics are also indicative of one who has accepted the prospects of "becoming" a self-directed human being.[21]

The Importance of Communication. In every human contact. something should be communicated. It has been agreed generally that communication by means of language is one of man's distinctive abilities. And yet it is observed that serious defects are apparent in the development of this ability both in the schools and in society at large.

It is not uncommon to hear educators and critics proclaim the need for improving the skills of reading, speaking, and writing. It must be remembered, however, that communication is a two-way process; to facilitate verbal communication, it may be at least as important to teach the art of listening as it is to teach reading. It has been said that "reasonable men always agree if they understand what they are talking about." Whereas people might not always agree, particularly when different values, attitudes, and emotions are involved, they could certainly communicate more effectively by developing their ability to listen, to understand the philosophies and values of others, and to recognize the importance of how any communication is perceived in both substance and process.

Educators have a considerable responsibility to help improve our methods of communication and to become cognizant of the necessity of more effective communication in today's world.

The Need for National Coherence. In America, there is educational need not only to help children and adults develop a conscious-

---

[20]Abraham H. Maslow, *Toward a Psychology of Being*, New York: D. Van Nostrand Co., 1962, p. 23.

[21]*See:* Abraham H. Maslow, *Motivation and Personality*, New York: Harper & Brothers, 1954.

ness of self and to grow to capacity and fulfillment, but also to achieve a societal coherence never fully manifested in the nearly two hundred years of our national history. This is true particularly of problems relating to segregation of and discrimination against minority groups.

An excellent recent article on the evils of segregation was written by a person who was blind and had experienced the frustrations which come from identification with a minority group. It was almost impossible for this blind man to find employment after completing his doctoral studies. The demon of self-doubt was planted in his mind. He started to question his own character and personality, to feel that perhaps there was a flaw, some defect or deformity that was obvious to everyone but himself. In relating his feelings on discrimination, he wrote:

> To admit that you are no better than other men is simple modesty.
> To admit that you are worse than they are, an inferior creature,
> a second-rate human being, is self-degradation. And yet this is
> what the color barrier demands of millions of American Negroes
> every day of their lives. The true evil of segregation is not exter-
> nal, but internal. It is the corrosive self-doubt that poisons the
> will, the gnawing sense of inferiority that eats at the soul.[22]

James Baldwin has written, "The whole root of our trouble, the human trouble, is that we will sacrifice all the beauty of our lives, will imprison ourselves in totems, taboos, crosses, blood sacrifices, steeples, mosques, races, armies, flags, nations, in order to deny the fact of death."[23] He further suggests that "everything white Americans think they believe in must now be re-examined."[24]

There might be more agreement with Baldwin if he were not only insistent on the fact of death, but also on the fact of life and what might be done to improve it. It would seem more noteworthy to re-examine much of what *all* Americans do, rather than what they profess to believe. The American articles of faith have always been lofty in declaration. Our educational system has been rather successful in teaching idealistic beliefs relating to acceptable standards of conduct. It is now necessary to help individuals develop the capacity for self-decision and to adopt codes of morality based on the consciousness of "right." Many of our rules for moral and social behavior were set forth by dead hands

---

[22] Peter Putnam, "If You Had a Choice," *Saturday Review*, October 26, 1963.

[23] *The Fire Next Time*, New York: The Dial Press, 1963, p. 105.

[24] *Ibid.*, p. 117.

of the past. It would seem appropriate to teach people a new concept of sanctionless morality based on the needs of the individual and of humanity. More than ever before, educational programs in the schools and colleges must produce men and women who can think and can find adequate solutions to formidable world problems.

The Abolition of War. The achievement of national coherence is imperative. A world existing in peace is likewise imperative. The survival of Western culture and indeed civilization as we know it will depend on at least two things: man must cultivate not only his intellectual and reflective faculties to the management of his own life, but he must also learn the management of group relationships at all levels of human organization. Group relationships are within man's ability to maintain and develop. "Human relations" is a subject and a process which can be learned.

In today's society, individuality must not be attained at the expense of one's fellows. Individuality might be achieved by cooperation, mutual aid, and common understandings about the goals each man wishes to attain.

> The democratic unit cannot function or long survive unless the individual selves first learn to govern themselves and to sacrifice some personal profits and preferences for the welfare of the group. This is altruism. Quite apart from any ethical considerations and in terms of strictly biological survival value, altruistic behavior marks the highest level of cultural evolution. It is a key factor, and the only one that can relieve the tensions that now endanger all the cultures of the world. This is not a speculative vagary or a fantasy of wishful thinking. It is validated by the whole history of human evolution and especially clearly by current events.[25]

The religious poet and philosopher have seen man as a special creation of the Deity, endowed with a spirit demanding self-fulfillment and ultimate perfection. The spirit and character of man are different from the component attributes of any other of the Creator's living creations. But even if one rejects the prospect of a divine creation or the general metaphysics of the idealist, the empiricist has noted observable phenomena which indicate the desire of the human spirit — human consciousness — to be free and eager to find meaningful purpose.[26]

---

[25] Herrick, *loc. cit.*

[26] *See:* Loren Eiseley, *The Firmament of Time*, New York: Atheneum Publishers, 1960.

In the last published work of C. G. Jung, the old man reflected on his memories, dreams, and observations. He wrote about the current issue with considerable realism.

> Natural history tells us of a haphazard and casual transforma-
> tion of species over hundreds of millions of years of devouring
> and being devoured. The biological and political history of man is
> an elaborate repetition of the same thing. But the history of the
> mind offers a different picture. Here the miracle of reflecting con-
> sciousness intervenes — the second cosmogony. The importance
> of consciousness is so great that one cannot help suspecting the
> element of *meaning* to be concealed somewhere within all the
> monstrous, apparently senseless biological turmoil, and that the
> road to its manifestation was ultimately found on the level of
> warm-blooded vertebrates possessed of a differentiated brain —
> found as if by chance, unintended and unforeseen, and yet some-
> how sensed, felt, and groped for out of some dark urge.[27]

The concept of human dignity emerges as the most important single factor between the success or failure of the entire human experiment. The concept of human dignity coupled with prospects of men living in peace throughout the world will be possible through the accomplishment of educational objectives transcending provincial philosophies. The concept of the perfectibility of man into some God-like being may be naïve. The prospects of learning to live with dignity, as human beings were meant to do, is possible and is not naïve.

THE TASKS AHEAD

Education is the best means we know to accomplish the individual and societal goals considered important and imperative in the world today. Criticisms may be leveled at the pupils, the teachers, or the schools, but these scarcely provide answers to the basic problems or help clarify issues. Protestations for freedom and peace are not enough. Calls for "quality education" and the search for "excellence" will remain clichés until such time as leadership among mankind charts a possible direction to the solution of problems dealing with the human being as a person and peace as a world necessity.

To teachers and other educators, the tasks are apparent. The heritage of centuries has been entrusted to them. The transmission of this heritage with its values and aspirations is a primary responsibility of all those who teach. But educational energies should not stop at this

---

[27] Jung, *op. cit.*, p. 339.

point. The focal point of education should remain that of helping man become free from the superstitions of the past, from the limitations to freedom imposed by societies which preceded him, and from anything alien to his human nature.[28] Education is more than a preparation for some future life; it offers a continuing model of what freedom might be and what the human being might become.

Have we really ever thought that in the classroom, a very small area in the expanse of the world, there is an opportunity to practice and teach about the freedom it has taken centuries and countless lives to achieve? In the classrooms of our schools and colleges, there is an opportunity to show that profound respect for freedom and dignity of another that must be transferred to the community and to the society.

We can believe in and accept the call for a more rigorous education. All men can do a better job in their calling. But contrary to the critics who denounce the efforts of teachers and the educational system in general, one might be proud of American education. American educators and the general citizenry should take encouragement from results already achieved, and yet remember that many goals of education still present problems.

Throughout the ages, mankind has struggled for the dignity of his being. But dignity and freedom do not come automatically; they are achieved by dedicated commitment and persistent effort. Our political freedom may have been won in the eighteenth century, but each man in each generation must win anew his moral freedom. Each man must achieve his own personal dignity. And to those persons who feel discrimination, education may be the best means to achieve self-dignity, freedom, liberty, and other conditions of life to which all men aspire. It is the responsibility of the teacher to find deeper meanings for freedom and to explore better ways to achieve national coherence and international peace. It is the challenge to the teacher to help pupils understand the potential of their existence in relationship to a common human destiny.

It is the challenge to all educators to help mankind find both dignity and freedom.

Hundreds of children will pass through the classroom of each American teacher as they attempt to find themselves and their niche in the world. In the school, they should hear of the "good life" and should be given the knowledge and skills to achieve it.

The laws of history may be stringent, and undoubtedly the chal-

---

[28] *See:* Algo D. Henderson, *Policies and Practices in Higher Education*, New York: Harper & Brothers, 1960, p. 24.

lenges are great. And yet one is reminded of that conversation between those two noted American educators, Charles A. Beard and George S. Counts, who were reflecting on the problems of the world and what man might do to solve them. It is said that Counts queried Beard concerning the laws of history. Beard thought for a moment, and replied, "Perhaps the laws of history are: (1) Whom the gods would destroy, they first make mad; (2) The bee fertilizes the flowers that it robs; and (3) The mills of the gods grind slowly, yet exceedingly small." Another day as these men continued their discussion, Beard suggested another possible law of history: "When it gets dark enough, you can see the stars."

Perhaps in the haste of this generation to accomplish so many things, we have suddenly been confronted with twilight. We cannot afford to remain complacent, and we cannot turn back. We can take courage from the fact that starlight is directly ahead, and that man can chart his direction from the knowledge and experience of the past and from the image of future goals. We can also know with surety that the sun is somewhere shining brightly, and that if our navigation is correct and faith in ourselves secure, we shall always see the dawning of the new day.

2. Trapped Concepts Impede American Education

IT HAS BECOME COMMONPLACE TODAY to be critical of certain aspects of American education. Indeed, the criticism may be justified, but fanatical attacks do not solve the many problems which have emerged in the mid-twentieth century. The American ideal of universal education remains an important concept and a worthwhile goal. To declare that American education has failed in providing certain needs for social adjustment, in giving all students universal knowledge of the liberal arts, or in developing the "other-directed" or "inner-directed" man is trite, even if true. The completion of formal educational programs does not guarantee that any person will achieve all of the diversified objectives considered important by all peoples. To assert, however, that modern educational opportunities, methods of instruction, and learning achievements are inferior to those of a yesteryear is foolish. Such criticisms are marks of an uninformed person. They are not substantiated in fact.

A minimal level of universal education, encouraged for a century by American educational leaders, may be achieved in the public schools during the twentieth century. The prospects of a universal higher education and the problems involved in providing it have not been considered until recently by American institutions of higher learning. Currently, the administrators and professors in American colleges and universities are frustrated by the numerical increase of students seeking admission. When questions of objectives and curricula are raised, the educator appears lost in a labyrinth of proselyting philosophies.

One of the great problems confronting the educator involves the proposition that man has a desire to learn, but that learning is impeded by psychological barriers. While it is true that man's ability to symbolize and to retain conceptual knowledge has permitted the development of formal educational programs, this ability may be thwarted by cultural demands and conceptual clichés.

American anthropologists have convinced us that the culture into which a baby is born will determine how the adult will think, feel, and act. It has been accepted generally that the culture will determine "what language [man] will speak, what clothes, if any, he will wear, and what gods he will believe in, how he will marry, select and prepare his foods, treat the sick, and dispose of the dead. What else could one do but react to the culture that surrounds him from birth to death? No people makes its own culture; it inherits it ready-made from its ancestors or borrows it from its neighbors."[1]

It is further observed that "education is a means employed by society in carrying on its own activities, in striving for its own objectives. Thus, during peacetime, society educates for peace, but when the nation is at war, it educates for war. In times of peace, munitions makers are 'Merchants of Death'; but when war comes, it's 'Praise the Lord and pass the ammunition.'"[2] Essentially, therefore, the level and intensity of education effort in any society reflect the needs of the society.

Universal education cannot be a panacea for the ills of modern society, nor can it reform society from the outside. The basic culture of a people must be changed from the inside. Education will reflect the changes desired or required by the culture. This does not mean that a planned educational program cannot intensify the interaction between man and his culture. It suggests, however, that among other things, "trapped concepts" promulgated and certified by the culture become barriers in the learning process of the individual and in the attempt toward general reconstruction of the culture. Indeed, it would seem that any education worthy of the name "liberal" must of necessity involve the person in the interactive process between a culture demanding acceptance of traditional patterns and new knowledge held by researchers, scholars, and/or educators.

While trapped concepts may impede man's learning process, man's ability to conceptualize is vital to his education. A concept is defined simply as an idea symbolizing the meaning of a universal nature and indicating comprehension of all essential attributes of a general class or logical species.[3] Man's ability to learn, to remember,

---

[1] Leslie A. White, *The Science of Culture*, New York: Grove Press Co., 1939, p. 337.

[2] *Ibid.*, p. 346.

[3] The author is aware of the operational definition of a concept. *See:* Percy Bridgman, *The Logic of Modern Physics*, New York: The MacMillan Co., 1927. "A concept is synonymous with the corresponding set of operations. If the concept is physical, as of length, the operations are actual physical operations, namely, those by which length is measured; or if the concept is mental, as of mathematical continuity, the operations are mental operations, namely those by which we determine whether a given aggregate of magnitudes is continuous."

In the current article, "concept" is used in a generic sense and includes metaphysical considerations. Indeed, many of the trapped concepts impeding education may be metaphysical rather than epistemological.

and to utilize both facts and concepts enables him to relate to a cultural system which develops on a base of inherited and accumulated knowledge.

Certainly the ability to remember has been as important to the development of cultural patterns as the ability to symbolize. Physiologically, the phenomenon of memory may be explained as a continuing activity, a trapped nerve message running round and round a particular set of loops formed by the synapses of two or more of the ten billion neurons in the brain.[4] Time must elapse between having an experience and fixing it in the mind. Experiments have suggested that time needed for memory fixation may well be occupied by nerve messages running around a neuron chain.[5] Only after enough passages have been made around the circuits involved is there a permanent change left in the neurons or synapses.

As the individual reacts to and assimilates sensory or cognitive experiences, there is continual transformation. Trapped concepts and stereotypes may develop through constant repetition and reproduction of conceptual abstractions. If such concepts are constantly reinforced, barriers to learning will be effected which tend to repel new concepts, new knowledge, and new behavior patterns. The designation "stereotype" has a negative connotation, but while a stereotype is a trapped concept, the latter may assume either positive or negative attributes depending on one's culture and communicative effectiveness. Many propositions of our educational, political, and social philosophies, which can be compared to the magic formulas held by primitive peoples, are trapped concepts. They may perhaps be useful in maintaining cultural *status quo*, but they are also responsible, in large part, for educational and cultural sterility.

Essentially, trapped concepts are charged with emotion. They represent biases and predispositions difficult to relinquish. The trapped concept has been called *truth* so often that it is believed, even if new knowledge supported by facts has disproved it.

It is the thesis of this paper that, while there is a possibility for individual man to achieve an education beyond and above the cultural demands of any given society, trapped concepts impede a liberal education. Although the proposition that education *per se* can directly change culture is discounted, it is certainly believed that education

---

[4] R. W. Gerard, "The Brain: Mechanism of the Mind," *An Outline of Man's Knowledge of the Modern World*, edited by Lyman Bryson, New York: McGraw-Hill Book Company, Inc., 1960, p. 79.

[5] *Ibid.*

can transform any individual having potential ability and a desire to rise above cultural expectations. Such a person could, of course, interact with his culture and in such interaction indirectly influence the development of culture.

American culture is demanding the spread and development of formal education. Education is being demanded as a panacea for the ills of society, and particularly as a means to outrun the technological progress of competitive societies. But education can also serve as a scapegoat, an excuse for not achieving those goals which, in effect, mankind is not yet ready to pursue and accept. Specifically, if the adult-dominant-status group of a culture were actually interested in developing the educational programs beyond cultural necessity, there would be more evidence of material wealth expended in this direction.

Hans Reichenbach observed, "The urge to knowledge is so deeply rooted in man that it can scarcely be omitted from a list of life's important needs."[6] This thought has been developed by many philosophers, political leaders, and educators. However, the educational question concerns the kinds of knowledge important to man. And the question has been answered generally only in terms of the culture or society in which it is asked.

Education in America originated as a continuation of the European plan of providing opportunities leading toward the abundant life for the privileged few. It developed into a system which aimed at providing growth and opportunities culminating in a rich and full life for everyone. Eventually more specific objectives were promulgated, suggesting that the educated person will have acquired behavior patterns indicating the attainment of self-realization, evidence of economic understanding, the assumption of citizenship responsibilities, and effectiveness in human relations. The American culture has demanded that the citizen reach a minimum level of behavior manifesting the pursuit and achievement of these goals.

Some professional educators have suggested that education has progressed to a point where mass intelligence is trained for the judging of human affairs. The fact remains that only individual man can achieve a personal education, cultivate his own intelligence, and transcend the limitations placed on his development by the general society and subcultures into which he is born. The trapped concepts of his culture will take precedence in his educational development. Only through persistent effort and motivated interest can any individual transcend the bar-

---

[6] *Atom and Cosmos* (translated in collaboration with the author by Edward S. Alien), London: George Alien & Universe Ltd., 1932, p. 16.

ren concepts which his culture insists are correct and important. And even if man is able to relinquish those concepts which have become sterile and unrelated to the development of cultural potential, and which may have little intellectual meaning for him personally, he will never be able to forget completely or ignore the demands of his original culture.

With respect to "education" itself, a trapped concept is evident. Many people assume that a certain body of correct knowledge and/or truth exists which can and should be learned by everyone. Although some progress is observed in reinterpreting the authoritarian structure of such epistemology, there has been little done at the university level to consider the capability of the students to understand the abstract concepts projected in nearly every field.

When is the individual student capable of evaluating the theories of economics, history, political science, philosophy, or any of the behavioral sciences? Even at the university level, is the student educated to an objective evaluation of the writings of Pareto, Dewey, Russell, or Freud? Such evaluation assumes that the student has had freedom to learn. In many schools, freedom to learn is trapped by demands to learn certain concepts which are deemed "right." Unless trapped concepts are penetrated, is the American college student any better prepared than the high school student, except by chronological maturity, to interpret "specific versus general evolution," "the organic theory of the state," or "American democracy"? Can the graduate student think critically and logically enough to answer his counterpart in the Soviet Union respecting the philosophy of "dialetical materialism"? Is the university student even prepared to understand himself as a person?

C. G. Jung has said:

> As a rule the individual is so unconscious that he altogether fails to see his own potentialities for decision. Instead he is constantly and anxiously looking around for external rules and regulations which can guide him in his perplexity. Aside from general human inadequacy, a good deal of the blame for this rests with education, which promulgates the old generalizations and says nothing about the secrets of private experience. Every effort is made to teach idealistic beliefs or conduct which people know in their hearts they can never live up to, and such ideals are preached by officials who know that they themselves have never lived up to those high standards and never will. What is more, nobody ever questions the value of this kind of teaching.[7]

---

[7] *Memories, Dreams, Reflections*, New York: Pantheon Books, 1963, p. 330.

This problem is more important than is generally assumed. How many professors in American colleges and universities are really interested in developing educational programs beyond the specialization required of majors in their own disciplines? How many teachers are really interested in encouraging educational achievement beyond the requirements of basic cultural expectations?

An anthropocentric illusion is a trapped concept inherent in the educational doctrines of Western civilization. Western man has continued to teach that which *should be*, without serious consideration for that *which is* or what *might be*. With his Graeco-Christian background, Western man has always placed the *ideal* on a much loftier plane than the reality of any logical analysis. Education has been proclaimed as the means by which perfection or the ideal can be attained. In some ways this proclamation has forced educators to compartmentalize theory and practice, admonition and behavior. Even if high ethical standards may be the very principles of a culture, progress toward them is not made by repeating clichés and conceiving them to be facts. It would seem more advantageous and certainly more reasonable to encourage students to learn and understand the reality of the cosmos as well as to aspire to personal goals of human perfection.

The "fact" that all men are created equal is supposedly understood by all secondary school pupils who have read and discussed *The Declaration of Independence*. Other immortal utterances of the founding fathers are always quoted to afford authority to this "truth." The fact that men are unequal in physical and intellectual capabilities and that society is built upon just such diversity cannot be used in a stereotyped study of our institutionalized life. In common usage, the proposition that all men are created equal is a trapped concept. It has been accepted as an educational slogan, particularly in political and social areas, and with enough repetition, the words are conceived as the substance.

The equality of man is not found in the words, but rather in the common humanity shared by all human beings. Man is a self-conscious being, and with his ability to symbolize, he might consciously seek personal goals as well as cultural ones. Man may also develop equality in the capacity to feel, and to relate his feelings to other human beings. In a positive sense, one can learn to love, and in cultivating this emotion, he comes to realize that by putting forth his hand, he might anticipate the touch and response of another person who cares. In such emotional understanding, there is an achievement of equality.

Where educational opportunities and rewards for distinctive achievement are offered to all individuals, man can become free as well as equal. He can, at least, free himself from superstition, prejudice, and dogmatism. Writing on liberal education, Algo D. Henderson has indicated the close relationship between equality and freedom.

> People are free insofar as they possess the tools of learning and techniques of action; the ability to verbalize, to calculate, to analyze and synthesize, to create, or organize, and to administer. People are free who possess, or know how to acquire, the available knowledge pertinent to the courses of action which they are undertaking at the moment. Persons are not free who are handicapped with unnecessary psychological inhibitions, who are the victims of preventable communicative diseases, who harbor irrational prejudices against men of different view or other cultures or races, or who practice religious bigotry.[8]

While men cannot be perfectly free or equal, they can achieve a degree of personal freedom within the bounds of a culture. Such a freedom should permit the assumption and development of personal responsibility and the acceptance of a moral code based on knowledge of the "good life" rather than on the fear of sanctions and eternal punishment.

But even if knowledge can contribute to freedom, there must be a definition of goals before educators can contribute constructively to society. The educational process consists partly in interpreting science to society, in liberating man from the superstitions of the past, and in penetrating the trapped concepts which hold man in darkness.

While our traditional education has interpreted the symptoms of schisms in society, it has evaded some of the real causes of human and societal breakdown. Science has projected theories into new frontiers of knowledge, indicating the great potential of man, but science must now recognize that man does not operate in a vacuum or in a test tube. Man lives within a cultural context.

Science has liberated man from some of the superstitions of the past and has developed logical and systematic methods of surveying and analyzing the *real* materials and relationships of the cosmos. Religion, on the other hand, has also made contributions to the development of human beings. Religion has posited an ideal which man may achieve at some future date. And although it has become fashionable to suggest that religion has not met the cultural or educational test of the current century, the indirect spiritual influence of the truly religious

---

[8] *Policies and Practices in Higher Education*, New York: Harper & Brothers, 1960, pp. 24–25.

person, although not enormous, undoubtedly contributes more to individual development than many people think.

But the baser attributes of man — aggression, hostility, and neurotic drives — still lurk in the background. They are scarcely known or understood by most of mankind. These less desirable traits of the human being are not of his nature, but of his experience. They are responsible, in part, for inadequacy in human relations, insensitivity to the disparities of human circumstances, and war and destruction among societies of man.

Pessimism is not the answer, and a cynic becomes a parasite who would destroy all progress, And yet we should ask ourselves: Is the *cosmic-onflow* of which Spengler wrote the most significant fact within the world-as-history? Perhaps we should ponder more carefully this statement: "World History is the World Court. Always it has sacrificed truth and justice to might and race, and passed doom of death on men and peoples in whom truth was more than deeds and justice more than power."[9]

It has been noted that people do not really *control* their cultures through education. On the other hand, culture is not a super-organism with a life of its own divorced from the behavior of men. The key to cultural progress is the interaction between man and culture.

To disavow the power of man, and particularly the educated man, in his ability to influence culture, can also become a trapped concept. Anthropocentrism and cultural determination become postulated ends of a historical, but theoretical continuum. In the dialectic suggested by the position of both concepts, each becomes sterile as an absolute of "truth." When one analyzes either education or culture, the interactive process becomes a more meaningful and fruitful locus for interpretation. Indeed, *process* is the reality, and cultural change through interaction the quality, of truth.

Men, capable of symbolizing, thinking, and feeling, capable of recognizing human uniqueness, must consider and concern themselves with trapped concepts which prevent human progress. Mankind has little reason to fear a real education. Those "truths" and traditions which are basic to the progress of man and humanity will emerge again and again, not as trapped concepts, but as evidences of objective reality. The dignity of man and the importance of his freedom stand as declarations of this fact.

---

[9] Oswald Spengler, *The Decline of the West*, Vol. II, New York: Alfred A. Knopf Co., 1930.

Education must become more than a profession, a concept of individual achievement, or a means of transmitting the culture. Education must remain the bulwark against the irrational action of those men who may be controlled by passion or motivated by selfish goals. To do this, educational programs should be divorced from slogans which entrap them and philosophies which limit their effectiveness. If a liberal education does nothing else, it should impart to men the knowledge that within the cultural framework, each individual is a person with considerable power of choice. Man must see himself as an agent of force in the society. Man must also understand himself and, with an understanding of his potential ability and his decision-making power, he might transcend any particular situation in any environment.

3. Responsibility For Educational Direction

THERE ARE MANY PROBLEMS confronting those persons engaged in directing and developing educational programs in America today. There are educational problems unique to various areas of the nation. There are the traditions and policies of the many institutions of education. There are the many opinions of the thousands of persons who complete formal educational programs and enter the teaching profession. And there are the diverse opinions of lay citizens with their own ideas about what is right and wrong, what needs to be done, and what procedures should be followed in solving these educational problems.

And yet, there is a common thread running throughout the nation at large which binds together into a cohesive group those professional and lay persons interested in education. Generally, many differences disappear when people learn of each other's philosophies, goals, and programs. Surprisingly enough, many persons find that they are on the same general team and seeking the same general objectives.

As one reflects upon the many and varied subjects which may be appropriate for discussion among educators today, the real challenges still seem to revolve around definitions of education, the processes of education, and the determination of "good" teachers and "good" schools. These topics may seem elementary and even commonplace; they have been subjects for discussion for two centuries. The discussion of these issues and the attempt to solve the resultant problems may in reality epitomize the conscious effort on the part of educators to assume responsibility for determining educational direction in America.

CONCEPTS AND PURPOSES OF EDUCATION

The concept of liberal education has always had great meaning for many Americans. The goal of liberal education has been defined as the outreach of the mind beyond the local prejudices and slavish venerations of the past to a broad understanding of the present and an anticipated future. In several studies on the subject, it has been suggested that a genuine liberal education cultivates at least three components of human thought and action: a generous knowledge of the major divisions of modern learning; effective use of skills of reasoning and communication; and such traits of character as intellectual curiosity, respect for other human beings, and a relatively stable set of values regarding man and the universe.[1]

In a generic sense, Nicholas Murray Butler's definition of education seems inclusive and constructive in its overtones. He suggests that "education is the acquisition of the spiritual possessions of the race." He explains that the term "spiritual possession" includes the great creations and accomplishments of mankind in the literary, scientific, institutional, aesthetic, and religious areas.[2] One cannot argue with the vision seen here, but one might enlage upon the definition as it might more appropriately apply to man in the mid-twentieth century. Education must mean more than transmitting the cultural heritage alone. We must do more than merely catch up with the human race. We must extend the boundaries of our present knowledge and find new knowledge and new skills to cope with problems previous generations have not encountered.

John Dewey's concept of education may well be the most meaningful of all. Dewey conceived of education as a process of living and not merely a preparation for future living. He also defined education as "a process of continuous reconstruction of experience with the purpose of widening and deepening its social content, where at the same time, the individual gains control of the methods involved."[3] One of Dewey's best definitions of education is found in the statement he entitled *My Pedagogic Creed*.

> All education proceeds by the participation of the individual in the social consciousness of the race. This process begins unconsciously almost at birth, and is continually shaping the individual's powers, saturating his consciousness, forming his habits,

---

[1]*See:* Earl J. McGrath and Charles H. Russell, *Are School Teachers Illiberally Educated?* New York: Bureau of Publications, Teachers College, Columbia University, 1961; Earl J. McGrath, *Liberal Education in the Professions*, New York: Bureau of Publications, Teachers College, Columbia University, 1959; R. Freeman Butts, *The College Charts Its Course*, New York: McGraw-Hill Book Company, Inc., 1939.

[2]Nicholas Murray Butler, *The Meaning of Education*, New York: Charles Scribner's Sons, 1902, p. 25.

[3]Ralph B. Winn, Editor, *John Dewey: Dictionary of Education*, New York: Philosophical Library, 1959, p. 32.

training his ideas, and arousing his feelings and emotions. Through this unconscious education the individual gradually comes to share in the intellectual and moral resources which humanity has succeeded in getting together. He becomes an inheritor of the funded capital of civilization. The most formal and technical education in the world cannot safely depart from the general process. It can only organize it or differentiate it in some particular direction.[4]

For those who work in professional education, there have been many lists published during the past half-century describing what the goals or purposes of American education should be. Educators recall the *Seven Cardinal Aims of Education* promulgated by the Commission on the Re-organization of the Secondary Schools in 1918. Following World War I, these aims were accepted by many progressive educators and laymen throughout the nation. The educator also remembers the *Ten Socio-Economic Goals of Education* and the *Ten Imperative Needs of Youth* published by other organizations during the past years. Each statement has contributed, in some way, to defining axiological aspects of a philosophy of education for America.

One of the better discussions concerning the purposes of American education was published by the Educational Policies Commission in 1938.[5] In this statement, it is suggested that the educated person should indicate accomplishments in the broad areas of (1) self-realization, (2) civic responsibility, (3) economic efficiency, and (4) human relationships. Although there is nothing in the outline form of these four areas which denotes literary magnificence, each statement is an excellent presentation of the goals to which the educated person in America might aspire. For example, the statement, "The educated person is sensitive to the disparities of human circumstances," underscores and acknowledges that education *per se* is more than individual intellectual achievement. Modern objectives of education suggest that the educated person should acquire more than self-realization — that he should learn behavior patterns which denote an understanding of "self" and an understanding of other people and of society in general.

Generally, certain trends may be observed in the development of our educational programs. In many ways, the unique contribution of American education to the world has been the "common school" idea which found its roots in New England. Moving westward with the

---

[4]*Ibid.*, p. 31.

[5]*The Purpose of Education in American Democracy*, Washington, D.C.: National Education Association, 1938.

frontier, the concept of the common school merged with the political theory of Jackson. And the justification of the political ideas of Jefferson, penned a half-century earlier, found substantiation in the equal chance provided by the common schools as they developed across the nation.

The aim of education is now based upon the possibility of providing a rich and abundant life for everyone rather than affording these opportunities to a selected artisocracy. Education also aims toward the development of the individual in relationship to society rather than in isolation. And it aims to help the individual not only to develop his intellect but achieve psychological and social satisfaction as well.

The success of American education must be observed in the attempt to develop the concept of universal education with all of its lofty goals. The world has noted that in this attempt there has been evidence of practice beyond verbalization alone. But there is a current imperative to redefine some basic objectives or purposes of education in America today.

Two additional and significant purposes of education may be observed in the need to help the student understand himself and to acquire a new interest in "moral" or ethical education. These needs and/or goals have been observed by many educational and lay leaders in America. These are not goals which will necessitate additional classes and compete for the hours of the school day but which should permeate the entire fabric of the educational system.

Those who have studied and contemplate how to improve conditions of mankind suggest that no science, no technique, no political constitution, no majority vote, and no specific educational practice, mechanical in itself, can reverse a major cultural trend which may be destroying us. Perhaps as one author has observed, "Our spiritual house has fallen in ruin, and we are floundering on the ground of a material wasteland."[6]

With respect to the objective suggestion that man must more than ever learn about the self, let us recognize that part of a person's struggle with life and with reason is his slow emergence from extreme dependency to a sense of mature perspective about himself and his culture. In substantiating this fact, one might cite the admonitions of the social and behavioral scientists, and those who practice the healing arts. The anthropologists, sociologists, psychologists, and psy-

---

[6] Robert Reynolds, "What Should be the Aims of the Public Schools?" Address before the Newton Connecticut Citizens Committee on Education, November 20, 1955.

chiatrists have brought to our attention repeatedly the need to examine carefully the real "human nature" of man, and in so doing to help him understand his needs, his limitations, his potential, and the unique dignity which affords him equality.

With respect to a renewed emphasis on moral education, it has been suggested again, even as the ancient prophets and philosophers proclaimed, that the mind of man has intuitive as well as practical means of achieving his destiny. It is with the development of moral and ethical standards that man may build a real spiritual house in which a child may dwell and learn in security and an adult may continue to grow in peace and satisfaction.

In the contemplation of both of these broad objectives, it will be necessary to acknowledge the insight of those persons who love life. As suggested by many writers, perhaps it will be necessary to live upon a foundation of reverence for life itself. When life becomes cheap, there is little satisfaction gained in learning about it. When it is revered, one finds new hopes and promises of fulfillment with each passing day. The self becomes important, not in egocentricity, but in acknowledgment of its value.

To teach children and adults a real understanding of self, and to teach a new but indeed self-disciplined morality entails the most difficult form of human work. The attainment of these objectives demands deep learning and labor. The major aims of education should really be directed toward accomplishments above and beyond many objectives caught in the current controversies of value hierarchy. These new objectives include an understanding of science, but also indicate that scientific knowledge is accumulative. Selfhood and morality must be learned anew by each generation and, more specifically, by each individual. Each person must learn what it means to be a human being.

WHAT IS INVOLVED IN THE EDUCATIVE PROCESS?

It would be foolish to assume that one might list all of the factors involved in the educative process. Certainly we agree that there is a body of knowledge about which teachers are expected to know and pupils are expected to learn. The relative importance of subject-matter mastery versus pedagogical techniques, however, is a fallacious argument to most educators. Any person who presumes to be a teacher must know the substantive content of his field or be considered incompetent. With respect to the educative process, however, three major factors may be considered. These are: (1) the teacher, (2) the pupils, and (3) the methods of teaching.

A teacher is envisoned as a person well educated and broadly informed about the society and world in which we live. He has substantial knowledge in a specialized field and is directly responsible for imparting this knowledge to his students. The teacher is a counselor as well as a director of learning. He is a professional person, and professionalism denotes an attitude of mind more than an acquisition of organization membership cards alone. The teacher is a person in his own right, but with acknowledgment that, in many ways, he is the personification of reality for the child.

The pupil is envisioned as a complex biological organism responding to the external stimuli which are offered in the various schools. He is also a self in his own right, bringing to the classroom a totality of being scarcely known by anyone, including himself. The pupil is a person with a quality transcending his biological structure alone. He is a human being, endowed with that unique characteristic of the race which will afford him the oportunity to use symbols to communicate his knowledge and feelings to other people. In perspective; the pupil is a person who will create unknown entities in the crucible of his potential experience.

Considering the various methods of teaching, one can only be suspicious of those in the profession who have found the one and best means of instruction. There are many different methods of teaching, each having value in consideration of time, place, and situation. Research findings verify such a statement. It is important that a teacher knows and understands various methods of teaching, but the real success in the classroom must rest with the significant planning of the teacher to attain his educational objectives.

The virtue of knowing and using various methods of teaching is to be found not only in helping pupils achieve higher scores on achievement tests, but also in helping them develop total behavior patterns, among which should be the cultivation of interest in educational pursuits. Essentially, the issue is an old one and merely suggests that the teacher should do more than acknowledge individual differences among pupils or be concerned with only one phase of development. The teacher should practice with the full realization that the total personality of the child is emerging in an educational setting.

There is a current call for "more rigorous" education. Such an education does not imply a return to reactionary organization and methods of teaching. Instead it implies the use of every technique and all information available to improve the standards of educational practice and production.

WHAT ARE GOOD TEACHERS AND GOOD SCHOOLS?

Some markings of a successful teacher have already been mentioned. When the adjective "good" is applied to an individual, there may be a connotation of morality or worthiness which is not always positive in evaluation. Some persons dislike determining the value and worthiness of other human beings. Thus, one should be more specific in evaluating the behavior and performance of the teacher in the classroom. An evaluation of "productive teaching" may be more appropriate and meaningful.

Beyond the need for substantive knowledge, both general and specialized, it would seem that the most productive teacher is one who has acquired several skills.[7] First, there are the technical skills involved in helping the pupil learn. Technical skills imply that the teacher knows various methods of teaching and can use them with different pupils in various situations. Second, there are human skills which acknowledge the feelings between two or more persons in any learning situation. In the cognizance of selfhood, the most effective teacher and/or administrator performs his task more efficiently if he understands the similarities of emotional responses among all human beings instead of assuming differences because of age or experience. Third, there are the conceptual skills sorely needed by all persons who presume to teach and direct the learning activities of others. Conceptual skills imply an understanding of the cause and effect relationship. A teacher with highly developed conceptual skills recognizes the importance of his calling. He may indicate in his own behavior, in his planning, and in his philosophy that the teacher may indeed affect eternity.

Superimposed on the requirements of knowledge and skills expected of the teacher are the general criteria, the cultural creed accepted by all thinking Americans. These criteria have been called ideals or principles.

1. Each person is of importance and of value as an individual.

2. All men should enjoy personal freedom.

3. All men should enjoy freedoms of speech, of assembly, and of worship.

4. All men should have the rights of security of person, equal protection before the law, and the right to petition the government.

---

[7]Although designations other than technical, human, and conceptual skills may be used, the author has used these categories as developed by Robert L. Katz in considering methods of administration. *See:* "Skills of an Effective Administrator," *Harvard Business Review*, Vol. 33, No. 1, January–February, 1955, pp. 33–42.

5. Each man is entitled to work and to live in the locality of his choice.

6. Each man has a right to manage his own affairs.

7. Each man may earn his living in a manner and in a place of interest to him.

8. The rights of any individual shall not interfere with the equal rights of other individuals.

9. Every individual owes obedience to the laws under which he lives.

10. The individual is responsible for himself and his family, and to the groups of which he is a member, to the nation, and to the world.

A "good teacher," if we must use the term, would personify these ten great ideals. Further, the "good teacher" manifests the *spirit of reverence*. Bertrand Russell has said:

> The man who has reverence will not think it is his duty to "mould" the young. He feels in all that lives, but especially in human beings, and most of all in children, something sacred, indefinable, unlimited, something individual and strangely precious, the growing principle of life, an embodied fragment of the dumb striving of the world. In the presence of a child he feels an unaccountable humility — a humility not easily defensible on any rational ground, and yet somehow nearer to wisdom than the easy-confidence of many parents and teachers. The outward helplessness of the child and the appeal of dependence makes him conscious of the responsibility of a trust. His imagination shows him what the child may become, for good or evil, how its impulses may be developed or thwarted, how its hopes must be dimmed and the life in it grow less living, how its trust will be bruised and its quick desires replaced by brooding will. All this gives him a longing to help the child in its own battle; he would equip and strengthen it, not for some outside end proposed by the state or by any other impersonal authority, but for the ends which the child's own spirit is obscurely seeking. The man who feels this can wield the authority of an educator without infringing the principle of liberty.[8]

As long as America is committed to the democratic philosophy the "good school" will admit all children who can profit by education in varying degrees. Whereas it is true that there cannot be a legal right to an education above and beyond the capacity of the individual to respond to an educational environment, there has been considerable effort on

---

[8] *The Basic Writings of Bertrand Russell*, edited by Robert E. Egner and Lester E. Denonn, New York: Simon and Schuster, 1961, p. 403.

the part of the schools to prepare children for an effective life as citizens of a democracy. Thus, there has emerged a moral right, a birthright established in America which precludes the transfer of these opportunities to an elite of any description. There has been insistent effort in America respecting the rights of the citizenry to determine, in some degree, who shall be the leaders in our society. Under such political theory, every citizen must have the most adequate education the public schools can design. This is the way the society perpetuates itself. Only in this way can leaders be educated and trained to understand the scientific, social, economic, and political issues confronting mankind. Only in this way can the political theory of today continue as acceptable for tomorrow.

The "good school" is staffed by the most qualified teachers it can acquire. These teachers are not only well educated themselves, but they are dedicated to a service of helping other persons learn and achieve. They not only adhere to the principle of individual differences, acknowledging that the growth patterns of children vary greatly, but they are fully aware of the fact that individual differences extend into adulthood to an even greater degree. These teachers also recognize that a slow pattern of growth is not an indication of the intelligence level inherent in the child. Many children with creative minds mature more slowly than other who may possess superior ability at the outset.

The research findings stemming from our institutions of higher learning substantiate these facts. In view of this research, who wants to decide, finally, who shall be educated?

The "good school" provides curricula which meet the needs of the pupils, the community, the state, and the nation. At the elementary level, the school should provide foundation curricula for all children. More than this, the school should provide an atmosphere which captures the interest of the pupils as they struggle to understand themselves and their environment. At the secondary level, the "good school" provides both college preparatory and terminal education programs. The "good school" is not involved constantly in controversy as to whether or not there are "frills in education," but rather offers instruction and experience in the fine arts, physical education, and social education, as well as in foundation courses for the humanities and sciences. To students unable to profit from higher education or unable to attend college, the "good school" offers a curriculum which may serve them well as they enter the labor market.

The "good school" provides facilities and equipment comparable to the demands placed upon it by the society it serves, considering both the present and the anticipated needs of the future. It is not enough for schools to operate with the facilities of a past decade if its students are expected to be equal to the present and competent to probe the demands of the future.

The "good school" provides library facilities which both inspire and fulfill the aspirations of the scholar. One can only be impressed with the observation of Wu Chow's Auntie in James Michener's *Hawaii*, when she wondered why the "ruling whites" allowed her children the opportunity to attend a school of any kind and learn how to read. To paraphrase her reflections: "Don't they know that once my children learn to read the printed page, they will become the leaders of their generation and of these islands?"

The "good school" provides an environment of experimentation and allows teachers the opportunity to apply research findings to the development of improved educational practice. The gap between research and application is inexcusable in many sections of the country. In many areas of the nation, educators have not been allowed to use the information at their disposal in the improvement of community educational programs.

The "good school" is a part of an organizational structure which affords the best possible means to use the professional competencies of the total staff. If the administration of education in the state and/or community is bogged down by archaic designs, what can be done is dictated by structure and not by intelligence, information, or function.

The "good school" provides institutional leadership to the community to the extent that it fuses the wisdom of the past, which has been proved necessary for cultural survival, and the new wisdom and technologies of the future into a meaningful pattern for the continued development and betterment of the body politic.

The American public has delegated a great responsibility to the schools but has failed to provide more than a fraction of the money necessary to discharge that responsibility. The fact that we spend more for entertainment, liquor, and other personal self-gratifying experience than we spend for education stands as an indictment against our culture. Someday we must face the fact that in many areas of the nation there are neither the buildings, equipment, nor the personnel to do a task which merits the services of the most qualified people and the best facilities.

The condition should long ago have been reason enough for all intelligent citizens to consider objectively the responsibilities and expectations of the "good school" and the various educational systems. Parenthetically, even the prestige of the professional educator has never been equal to the contributions made in local communities. The real unsung heroine of American public education may be the elementary teacher, who must spend her days, and many nights, working with little "potential plasticities" as they begin their evolution into the men and women of tomorrow. The monument to the public school teacher cannot be observed in the research papers and professional publications stemming from colleges and universities. The real monument must remain the successful and educated citizen of today, who was the child in the class of yesterday.

The issue has been well stated in the words of a noted American educator:

> Only the combined intelligence of many creative minds will solve the baffling problems confronting American education today. They cannot be solved by loudly braying the issue with no evidence in fact or an iota of ingenuity. Facts must remain the basis of consideration for any improvement in education. Misinformation, bias, ignorance lead to no better results in education than in any other human endeavor. It is perfectly obvious that any society which permits less than the most able to teach its children is committing national suicide. Those who almost gleefully point to the inadequacy of many of those who teach are displaying the most blatant, vulgar, sadistic ignorance of the possible relationship of education to human progress.[9]

Any thinking teacher or professor who views that total task of education, which involves social attitudes, value patterns, volumes of information, creative insights, and numerous skills, should feel a high sense of humility for himself and his colleagues. And any thinking citizen should be cognizant of the great responsibility assigned to the teaching corps in perpetuating our way of life.

A final question may be asked: As teachers and administrators, as professional leaders in our communities and in our various institutions, what kind of persons are we? Have we developed a philosophy of education, a personal philosophy of life, which will wear well through the months ahead? Are the messages we speak and the instruction we give consistent with the ideals we preach and the behavior we manifest?

More than anything else, teachers might well heed that ancient admonition, "Know thyself." Educators need to rely less on the sanctions imposed by the organization or the fleeting inspiration received from the leadership admired. Too often, when one is inspired, he

---

[9] The author is indebted for the above quotation to the late Professor Samuel J. McLaughlin, University of Utah.

merely suggests that he will do better or assumes that the words of encouragement apply to others than himself. Really, it is not necessary to say that one will do a better job of teaching, Rather than say it, one need only to do it.

With all due respect to those persons of authority who have made brief studies and then reported to the nation concerning the status of public education, it is suggested that in a short period of time, one cannot tell precisely what kind of education is to be found in the various American communities. Certainly there is need to evaluate our present-day programs, but we must not lose sight of the fact that our historical record speaks rather highly for what has already been accomplished through American education. It is a challenge to be concerned about charting the educational direction of tomorrow.

History alone indicates that nothing less than the "best" education should be found in every community in America. Professional educators must assume to a large degree the responsibility for charting educational direction for the people whom they serve. But the leaders of other institutions and organizations in our pluralistic society, indeed in theory all citizens, must also assume responsibility for the success or failure in attaining the educational objectives considered important for both individual and national survival.

Ultimately, is there anything more important that a "good" education? Some philosopher once said. "Education pre-occupies the unwritten page of being, producing impressions for the human type which only death can obliterate." Even on this latter point, one cannot be sure.

American education is still an idea as well as a process. Education mingles with the dreams parents have for the success of their children. Education weaves into history much of what shall be read in the generations to follow. The teacher, professor, and administrator have freely entered into the profession. Perhaps these educators cannot move mountains, but in a small, imperceptible, and significant way, educators can leave the world a little better than they found it.

4. Education and the Goals of Mental Health

IN RECENT YEARS, the subject of mental health has been of great concern to many individuals and social groups. Countless statements and briefs have been written indicating that mental illness remains a serious blight on our society. In some ways, it seems presumptuous to write another paper on the goals of mental health. Perhaps what is really needed is less presentation of the subject and more action by an informed citizenry to correct the situations which impede the prospects of better mental health for everyone.

Certainly, current research and educational direction have indicated the need and concern of the nation for the development of improved mental health programs.

FACTS, FIGURES AND PROGRAMS

It has been said that mental illness and mental retardation are among the most critical of the nation's health problems.[1] "They occur more frequently, affect more people, require more prolonged treatment, cause more suffering by the families of the afflicted, waste more of our human resources, and constitute more financial drain upon both the Public Treasury and the personal finances of the individual families than any other single condition."[2]

There are over one million persons suffering from mental and nervous disorders in the United States. In 1960, there were over 600,-000 persons hospitalized because of mental disorders, and it is estimated that over one half of the patients using the approximately 1,800,000 hospital beds in America today may require such hospitalization because of mental or psychosomatic illness.[3]

---

[1] Message from the President of the United States Relative to Mental Illness and Mental Retardation, 88th Congress, 1st Session, Document No. 58, House of Representatives, February 5, 1963.

[2] *Ibid.*, pp. 1–2.

[3] *See: Handbook on Programs of the U.S. Department of Health, Education, and Welfare*, Washington, D.C.: United States Government Printing Office, 1962.

It is also known that every year nearly 1,500,000 people receive treatment in institutions and hospitals for the mentally ill and mentally retarded. Speaking of these people, the late President Kennedy said: "Most of them are confined and compressed within an antiquated, vastly overcrowded, chain of custodial State institutions. The average amount expended on their care is only $4 a day — too little to do much good for the individual, but too much if measured in terms of efficient use of our mental health dollars. In some states, the average is less than $2 a day."[4]

The total cost of treatment for the mentally ill and mentally retarded is staggering, and yet insufficient in view of the magnitude of the problem. The total cost to the taxpayers is over $2.4 billion a year in direct public outlays for services. About $1.8 billion is spent to combat mental illness and $600,000 is spent on programs for the mentally retarded.[5] Besides the expenditures of the federal and state governments, there are additional outlays by organizations and foundations for mental health programs, as well as specific expenditures for mental health research and patient care in various mental hospitals. Naturally the cost per patient treated varies from state to state, but even the state affording the current highest amount is not expending enough. The Joint Commission on Mental Health has noted that on a daily basis, per patient maintenance costs from state to state range from $2.67 to $8.74. The cost of patient care in a general hospital averages about $32.23 per day. Financial surveys have indicated that mental health services have been short-changed or otherwise poorly supported and underfinanced in nearly every state.[6]

Indeed, mental illness is expensive in terms of money, buildings and facilities, professional services, and, most of all, human suffering. It is encouraging whenever proposals are made to help alleviate some of the problems related to mental health and to improve this aspect of the nation's well-being.

At least three additional means have been suggested for launching a new mental health program. The nation might: (1) establish comprehensive community mental health centers; (2) strengthen the therapeutic services of state mental institutions and encourage these institutions to undertake intensive demonstration and pilot projects concerning treatment of mental illness; and (3) engage in new pro-

---

[4]*See: Facts on Mental Health and Mental Illness*, Washington, D.C.: Public Health Service Publication, No. 543, March, 1962.

[5]*Message from the President, op. cit.*

[6]*See:* Rashi Fein, *Economics of Mental Illness*, New York: Basic Books, Inc., 1958.

grams of research dealing with mental processes, therapy, and other phases bearing upon mental illness.[7] With improved health programs and essentially broader education, the number of patients under custodial care might be reduced by 50 per cent within the next decade or two. More importantly, with additional research, proper education, and more adequate treatment, preventive measures might be taken to reduce the number of patients needing hospitalization for mental illness. Better medical care in general, improved educational programs in particular, and elevated social and economic conditions might conceivably enable scores of people heretofore considered hopeless to achieve mental health.[8]

Programs of mental health sponsored by the federal government may be important, but should not be considered as pioneer or exclusive. Various churches, philanthropic associations, local hospitals, and some local governments have been concerned with mental health programs for many years. The impact of these more isloated programs will probably never be as effective as would a national program supported by the federal government. The complexities of the problem and the resources needed to solve the many facets of mental illness suggest that federal government leadership and financial support are imperative.

Besides the federal government and the institutions already involved with the problems of mental health, the schools are in an excellent position to develop constructive programs in this field. The schools have a captive audience, and could foster in young people an understanding of the various aspects of mental hygiene together with an appreciation of the urgency of seeking treatment should one become emotionally or mentally ill.

It is significant to think of the millions of students in the elementary and secondary schools, the number of teachers employed, and the potential threat of mental illness in view of the anxieties and frustrations created by our fast-moving civilization.[9] Indeed, the school itself, with constant and increasing pressures upon scholastic standards and intellectual achievement, adds to the frustrations of many children who are not motivated to the academic pursuits or in some cases not able to benefit from college-preparatory curricula.

---

[7] Message from the President, *op. cit.*

[8] *Ibid.*

[9] *See:* Nelson B. Henry, Editor, *Mental Health in Modern Education*, The Fifty-fourth Yearbook of the National Society for the Study of Education, Chicago: University of Chicago Press, 1955.

In 1965, there were 53,300,000 sudents enrolled in elementary and secondary schools in this nation, 36,000,000 of them in elementary schools. There were 1,964,000 teachers employed to instruct children and supervise the many educational programs being offered. The estimated number of persons per 100,000 population requiring help for mental health problems can be determined statistically at any one time. In consideration of the large number of the nation's children in public schools, such a statistic is most significant in any determination of need for incorporating programs of mental health within the curricula.

According to information available from the U.S. Department of Health, Education, and Welfare, there were 208,000 children under the age of eighteen who received treatment in outpatient psychiatric clinics in 1959.[10] About 37,000 of these children were diagnosed as having personality disorders, either of a transient or a long-term nature. There were 801,000 juvenile court delinquency cases reported in 1962. These cases involved children between ages ten and seventeen.[11] It is believed that many of these cases relate to personality problems and are symptomatic of poor mental health. Certainly, many of these delinquency cases involve the failure of adolescents to find themselves in a society imposing increased social demands, responsibilities, and expectations.

It is impossible to determine precisely the number of children in the school-age population who are in need of psychiatric treatment or special counseling services, but the indication is that some 10 per cent is in need of professional intervention because of mental or emotional illness or maladjustment. Because of an inability to function "normally," another 10 per cent of the children is in need of counseling in school and sympathetic understanding in the neighborhood and at home.[12] It is known from observation and experience that there are many children who suffer from personality disorders and live from day-to-day without much opportunity to learn of reasons for their deviant behavior or to obtain insight concerning required behavior. Many of these children have known nothing but punishment for deviant behavior. They respond only with hostility to disciplinary action on the part of any adult acting in a role of authority.

---

[10] *Facts on Mental Health and Mental Illness*, Washington, D.C.: Public Health Service Publication, No. 543, March, 1962.

[11] *Key Facts on Health, Education, and Welfare: 1952 and 1962*, Washington, D.C.: United States Government Printing Office, 1963.

[12] Warren T. Vaughn, "Children In Crisis," *Mental Hygiene*, Vol. 45, No. 3, July 1961, pp. 354–359.

Francis C. Braceland has observed:

> Each individual has within himself a certain potential for mental health or mental illness and this is dependent upon a complex of biological, psychological, and sociological forces which affect his behavior. That man also is aided by his spiritual beliefs, declared or undeclared, is apparent to the careful observer. These forces impinge upon man's basic character, which has been shaped and moulded since his birth by family and environmental experiences, and some of these are stressful in the extreme.[13]

That mental illness is a potential obstruction to the optimum functioning of the individual is apparent. The inauguration of preventive programs in the schools should prove to be one positive solution.

Although specific programs have been established in many schools as "special education for the mentally retarded," there has been little concerted effort to develop programs of positive mental health for all school children. Other than the Detroit School Mental Health Project, few school teachers or districts have developed significant programs for teachers to learn about the subject or to become involved in helping the apparently "normal" child achieve goals of mental health.[14] It is merely assumed that children should attend school, complete a program of studies considered important by school authorities and the public, and, by such achievement, be able to enter the adult society and live in peace with themselves and with the world.

Victims of mental illness may be classified into three main categories: (1) those who are mentally defective, (2) those who have organic disorders stemming from physical or chemical anomalies, and (3) those with functional disorders.[15] This latter classification may be further divided into the psychotics and neurotics whose illnesses are presumed to originate in the mind. In many cases, however, the disorder cannot be ascribed to a demonstrable cause.

It is with those students who may develop the functional disorders that programs of mental health become particularly important. Whereas mental illness concerns a study of abnormal psychology, mental health is a subject and condition of concern to all "normal" people, including the "normal" and "average" student in our schools. It

---

[13] Public lecture delivered in Hartford, Connecticut. *See:* The *Hartford Courant*, May 14, 1963.

[14] Paul T. Rankin and John M. Dorsey, "The Detroit School Mental-Health Project," *Mental Hygiene*, Vol. 37, April, 1953, pp. 228–48.

[15] An excellent summary of basic facts in abnormal psychology for teachers was written by E. C. Hall. *See:* "What the Teacher Should Know about Psychiatry," *Progressive Education*, Vol. 31, No. 2 ,November, 1953, pp. 54–57.

is for these people that an understanding of the goals of mental health is especially significant.

The question might be asked therefore: What are the goals of mental health, and how might they be more effectively incorporated into the curricula of the schools? How might the educator exert more leadership in solving problems of mental illness and mental retardation and, indeed, promote better educational programs for any handicapped person?

WHAT IS MENTAL HEALTH?

There is a problem of defining mental health. As the term is used generally, mental health considers both "positive mental health" and "mental illness." Positive mental health must be observed as a condition wherein behavior is recognized as amenable to the realization of the individual potential.[16] There is a quantitative goal of mental health in the enhancement of self-realization for as many persons as possible. Generally speaking, however, goals of mental health refer to those conditions wherein certain elements of character and behavior seem manifest and important to the well-being of the individual and of society at large.

There are several key attributes of personality and character ascribed to those persons assumed to possess sound mental health. The following qualities or goals are cogent and rather inclusive: [17]

1. *Objective judgment:* This attribute suggests the ability to look at all kinds of facts squarely and accurately, neither overlooking some nor exaggerating others. This ability is also called rationality, good sense, and even common sense.

2. *Autonomy:* This is the ability to deal with daily events in a self-starting, self-directing manner. Such terms as initiative, self-direction, and emotional independence are often used to convey this idea.

3. *Emotional maturity:* This is the ability to react to events in a self-directing manner with emotions which are appropriate in kind and in degree to the objective nature of any situation.

4. *Self-realizing drive:* This is the habit of working hard and purposefully to one's full capacity. People vary greatly in their physical, intellectual, and social potentialities, but it is possible to see in each case

---

[16]*See:* Marie Johoda, *Current Concepts of Positive Mental Health*, New York: Basic Books, Inc., 1958.

[17]Robert F. Peck and James V. Mitchell, *Mental Health*, Washington, D.C.: National Education Association, 1962, pp. 3–4.

how far the given individual is putting his own particular potentialities to work to achieve worthwhile results. His powers, of course, are delimited by the degree and state of his development and by the opportunities he has had.

5. *Self-acceptance:* The acceptance of self is manifested in a positive attitude toward one's self. Conscious self-insight or self-understanding may not be absolutely essential to an attitude of self-acceptance, but either seems to enhance considerably the objectivity and the wisdom of a person's self-regard.

6. *Respect for others:* This denotes a positive accepting attitude toward other people.

Essentially, a person manifests mental health when he has accepted a concept of reality and has adopted and lives within a framework of values, beliefs, and commitments which might be called a philosophy of life. A philosophy of life, accepted and understood, serves as a foundation for living and may promote self-awareness considered important in achieving and maintaining mental health. Although a person may be skeptical of his philosophy at times, he does not stop functioning because of doubt, but moves forward on faith. Wayland F. Vaughn has said:

> The healthy-minded individual is likely to accept the following credo as a minimum (1) that the universe is basically good, that justice, therefore, will ultimately prevail; (2) that life is worth living; (3) that there is order in the universe; that events accord with definite principles which can be discovered and applied by the human mind, that life can be good if we work with and accept nature; (4) that the good life is one inspired by love and guided by wisdom. If a person can proceed further and believe in a loving heavenly Father, in the efficacy of prayer, in immortality, so much the better, if he does not sacrifice his integrity in embracing such beliefs.[18]

Whether or not teachers are concerned about mental health should not be an issue for debate. The goals of mental health are important to teachers personally, and they should know that it may be as important for all mankind to achieve these goals as it is to develop skills and acquire other forms of knowledge.

In many ways, the etiology of mental illness may be traced to

---

[18] *Personal and Social Adjustment*, New York: The Odyssey Press, 1952, p. 17.

problems arising in infancy and childhood. Indeed, mental health may depend upon the way the child is prepared for and introduced to the culture and society in which he will live. Adjustment to this culture must be accomplished without sacrificing the important concept of "individual rights and worth" observed important in the national ideology. There must be continual emphasis placed on the individual or on the consequences of individual action, on the need to assume individual moral responsibility, and on the need to develop a faith manifesting a willingness to attempt achievement of the goals set by self and by society. Considerable responsibility is given to the teacher in that he must teach the ideals of the cultural philosophy and also teach that there are obligations, restrictions, and demands required of the adult citizen in a democracy. Without adequate explanation, and certainly without adequate understanding of "rights and responsibilities," many pupils face a contradiction when entering the social interaction within the school-community and society.

All children face the stresses and strains of new social experience. Anthropologists have indicated that this is true in all cultures and not merely in our own.[19] Indeed, a part of "growing-up" and most of the process of maturation consist of learning to cope with the ambiguities of human existence to the extent that the child emerges as a "self" in his own right, independent of infantile ties and authoritarian direction. Most children accept and learn to cope with the necessary behavioral controls required in going along in the group and in community life. It is those children who fail to make the adjustment, who fail to respond to rules of acceptable personal and social behavior, with whom we are most vitally concerned in promoting more adequate programs of mental health.

In summary, the goals of mental health suggest that one should achieve understanding of the self, the ability to share one's self with other people, the ability to face reality, the capacity to tolerate reasonable tension, and the evidence of emotional maturity. To include these objectives with other purposes of schooling and/or formal education is to instruct the young in subjects as important as those which transmit information about the cultural heritage.

Is it too much to ask that teachers also become agents of promoting positive mental health? What should be the role of the teacher in helping pupils acquire mental health?

---

[19] M. K. Opler, Editor, *Culture and Mental Health*, New York: The Mac-Millan Co., 1959.

THE ROLE OF THE TEACHER IN HELPING
PUPILS ACHIEVE MENTAL HEALTH

Historically the teacher has dealt with the intellectual life of the students, but in the past few decades teachers have also become concerned with the total growth and development of the child. Surprisingly, mental health, so directly related to the mind and to educational achievement, has become only recently a subject of interest to the teaching profession.

Teachers of elementary and secondary school children observe many examples of deviant behavior and symptoms of maladjustment. Historically it was believed that the answer to these problems might be found by giving more and harsher discipline. Not many years ago, the success or failure of a teacher was measured as much by the appearance of disciplined children in the classroom as by the results of achievement tests and other educational accomplishments.

The overall objectives of education have been expanded considerably, and teacher-education programs now refer to a philosophy which presumes to understanding the child as a human being rather than as a "miniature adult" available for enforced intellectual feeding.[20]

Teacher-education programs today include much more than a study of pedagogical techniques and admonitions to make sure that children are properly disciplined. In most of the larger universities, prospective teachers are required to complete a regular program of studies in the liberal arts and sciences, as well as an academic major in a field of teaching specialization. Teachers are also required to complete formal study in educational psychology with emphasis upon human learning, personality development, and stages of human growth. Teachers are required to develop human skills and group techniques. The teachers of today also have learned how to use audio-visual equipment and facilities and many other instructional devices designed to enhance the learning of the children. Elementary and secondary school curricula today give greater consideration of the realities of life. The curricula are devised for the children and not for adults who fail to observe that reality for the child is different from that perceived by older people. Education and life are considered coterminous for the children. If this philosophy did not prevail, the ideals and values allowed to flourish in the children's minds would find contradiction

---

[20]*See:* I. N. Thut, *The Story of Education*, New York: McGraw-Hill Book Co., 1957, pp. 133–34.

between what is taught in the school and what is observed in the society.

Despite all of these developments, however, there remain those negative criticisms which suggest that schools should return to the practices and educational philosophies of a time gone by. It is suggested by some that schools should be concerned only with the cultivation of the intellect and the inculcation of habits denoting proper disciplined behavior.

There are also those persons who suggest that the schools should assume more and more responsibility for the care, instruction, and well-being of the child. To the critics who demand a return to the past, one can only say that social progress and research have indicated that the traditionalism and emphasis of a former generation are not sufficient. If we were to return to the specific kinds of education suggested by many critics, we would have schools only for the intellectually elite, and in view of the national philosophy such schools would not be adequate. Perhaps even women would find themselves hard put to defend the educational opportunities they have won in the past century if we were to abolish our comprehensive educational programs.

Universal education has become as important a tenet of American democracy as is the belief in the dignity and worth of every human being. This does not mean that every child has a right to a "higher education" or to any specific kind of educational program. There can be no right to an education *per se*. There can be opportunities provided every child for positive response toward an educational program of value to the determination of self-realization. Generally speaking, the society has accepted this position.

With respect to teachers assuming more responsibility for the overall achievement and total development of the child, the prospects of improving programs of positive mental health seem important.

The role of the teacher has been expanded. The teacher of today is required to be more than a repository of knowledge and a disciplinarian. The teacher's primary task will always be to teach; today's teacher, however, must also encourage the student to use his mind, help students think logically and objectively, and be concerned with the total growth and development of the child as he strives toward individual potential. Ostensibly, this expanded role suggests that good teaching is related to an understanding of the personality of the students. And, with such understanding, there might well be help afforded in resolving mental and emotional conflicts which arise in all human beings.

Teachers must develop greater understanding and must try to respond in a more positive way to those perplexing questions students ask about philosophy and religion. These questions always arise when the child moves from the sheltered family influence to the broader existence observed in the classroom culture and in society. In many ways, the teacher must walk a tightrope in being honest while affording answers to questions concerning the multitudinous beliefs of the nature of man and the universe. The teacher must defend the right of people to hold many diverse beliefs.

The teacher must do a better job of counseling pupils to see life's work integrated more closely with individual ambitions, interests, and talents. Teachers must be more expressive in their instruction. In some ways, the teacher becomes the personification of reality for many children, and he must, therefore, set an example, the worth of which is probably much greater than realized.[21]

Dana M. Farnsworth has said:

> In our schools and colleges, mental health education is almost inseparable from good education. In practice, there is nothing to be gained by making an artificial separation. Knowledge of mental health principles should be considered fundamental in the training of all teachers. Attention to them should serve not to burden still further an already overloaded curriculum, but to enable students and teachers alike to work for higher standards of academic and personal excellence.[22]

But there is less need for constant reiteration of the word excellence in intellectual pursuits alone. Those children who cannot excel scholastically become frustrated and anxious as they attempt to find other values which are considered important by their teachers. Are there not other achievements worthy of excellence? There is more need for consideration of excellence in *becoming* the kind of person the child might become as he moves toward self-realization with whatever qualities and abilities he is endowed. Excellence must be considered as a process rather than as a condition or substance equated to intellectual superiority.

Douglas M. Knight remarked:

> To excel, after all, is to go beyond, to thrust ourselves forth from where we are. But crucial questions remain; do we "go beyond" in the sense merely to project ourselves into the void?

---

[21] Dana M. Farnsworth, "Mental Health Education: Implications for Teachers," *Teacher's College Record*, Vol. 62, No. 4, January, 1961.

[22] *Ibid.*, pp. 272–73.

Are we concerned to go beyond others, such as Sammy runs perpetually until he drives himself to the point of exhaustion; or do we mean to go beyond ourselves so that we gain rather than lose, so that we are discoverers rather than fugitives? Until we begin to answer questions like these, the pursuit of excellence is nothing but a chase; *excellence* is as much a word of action as pursuit, after all; it is not a goal, it is merely (and at least) a means; it is not a word of substance, but a word of process. And important as the processes of life are, they mean nothing without the ends of life, the ends which (if they are valid) can never be reached, but can define and make firm some substance for words like *excellence, quality*, and *achievement*.[23]

It is assumed that most teachers today accept the principle that behavior is caused and is therefore subject to understanding and to redirection. It is also assumed that most teachers recognize that cultural conditioning is reflected in the child attending school. Essentially the child is faced sometimes with prospects of adjustment to an enlarged universe of reality. Our concern for adjustment is not with the *status quo*, but rather with the recognition of social facts and with an understanding of the horizon of better social existence.[24] Indeed, as noted above, the foremost objective of mental health is the ability to understand, interpret, and otherwise confront reality. While it is true that the psychiatrist may define reality as whatever it is plus one's perceptual assumptions about it, there is a normal process of maturation and sophistication which comes from educational experience. This experience should afford the development of perceptual abilities of the young child to the extent that whatever is presumed to be reality by the infant, based upon much fantasy and myth, changes to a more adult and objective interpretation of a pluralistic universe.

There can only be reiteration here that the teacher should not become a therapist in the sense of providing professional psychological or psychiatric treatment to pupils. But teachers, along with doctors, social workers, nurses, judges, probation officers, and ministers, are all professionals concerned with promoting sound mental health. Each profession has its own emphases, techniques, and spheres of operation. The overall objectives of these professions may overlap, and if the professional groups involved understand a common body of knowledge concerning the human being and employ a common understandable

[23] "Beyond Excellence," in *Addresses Given at the Annual Conference on Higher Education in Michigan*, University of Michigan Official Publication, Vol. 61, No. 80, January 1, 1960, pp. 36–46.

[24] *See:* Peter Blos, "Aspects of Mental Health in Teaching and Learning," *Mental Hygiene*, Vol. 37, No. 4, October, 1963, pp. 555–69.

terminology, there will be more concentrated action toward solving problems of mental illness. Certainly, there will be the establishment of better mental health programs in the public schools.

Recently, a teacher attending a university summer session class submitted a paper on how the teacher can help the emotionally disturbed child.[25] This teacher reflected upon her own role and upon the importance of her work in helping children. Almost poetically, she indicated the belief that what happens in the classroom will, to some degree, affect not only the future of the children, but the future of America as well.

As this teacher documented her statements and finally concluded her paper, she called for a self-examination. Her remarks are insightful. Among other things, this teacher wrote:

> This summer's classwork, the hours spent in the library, the writing and research that have gone into this paper would all be marked off as wasted unless some positive results take place next year. The following notes to myself will be a quick referral, an examination of conscience, a nudge, a spur.
>
> 1. Show each child that you respect and love him.
>
> 2. Be patient.
>
> 3. Be alert for clues to behavior.
>
> 4. Praise whenever possible.
>
> 5. If you must censure, do it privately and constructively.
>
> 6. Plan with the children.
>
> 7. Listen more than you speak.
>
> 8. Find time for private talks with the children.
>
> 9. Help each child to like himself.
>
> 10. Don't be too hard on yourself when you don't do all these things. You're human, too.
>
> I have no doubt that there will be days next year when I will be cranky, impatient, and bossy. The thirty-five youngsters before me will seem like so many little fiends, skilled in the more refined arts of torturing teacher. When I come home I will be too exhausted and disgusted to look at any books on children's needs or to recall the contents of this paper; but if I'm lucky, I

---

[25] Cornelia Reagan, *How the Teacher Can Help the Emotionally Disturbed Child*, Lexington: Bureau of School Service, College of Education, University of Kentucky, April, 1963.

will take a minute to glance at my notes to myself and decide to reread and try them out again just one more time tomorrow.

The next morning (if I've gone to bed on time) I'll go back to the classroom savoring teaching for the varied, exciting, creative job it is. My children will forgive me, for eight-year-olds seldom hold a grudge, and we will begin once more the ancient, difficult, and complex work of knowing and loving one another.

There are many attributes of the "good" or productive teacher not always considered in most general evaluations. Most of those people whom we think about in our own experience as "good" and influential teachers have demonstrated, among other qualities, emotional maturity and a considerable degree of self-understanding. In a sense, the successful teacher has also been searching for self, and has attempted to understand his personal motives, feelings, aspirations, and behavior. The search for self on the part of the teacher lends itself well to encouraging and helping students find their niche in the world.

In a recent novel by Allen Whellis, there is a story of a psychoanalyst's search for his own life's meaning.[26] The "seeker" speaks for teachers, pupils, and for all mankind as well as for himself. Essentially, the person is concerned with finding the self. The book notes that there must be a substantive meaning of the phrase "identification with the life process" and suggests that serving the needs of others is perhaps the whole meaning of life. The philosophy is not unlike our Western religious philosophy which has been important to many people for many centuries.

The "seeker" concluded his search by saying:

> As soon as you begin to care for people, you are swept along by your caring. Their needs won't wait, will not fit neatly into your pre-arranged schedule; but if you care you will forget what you are doing and try to help.... This is what life consists of and I am glad to have lived. I have been helped by others, and I have in turn given help to others. The lives of other men have held meaning for me, and my life holds meaning for them. I have had a place in the life process — biologically by being the son of my parents who are dead and the father of my children who live, and socially by contributing something to the ongoing work of civilization.[27]

Teachers might find that the philosophy of the "seeker" could hold great meaning for them in relation to their pupils. Indeed, life and the teacher really come to terms under the framework of service.

---

[26] *The Seeker*, New York: Random House Publishers, 1960.
[27] *Ibid.*, p. 227.

In the twentieth century, the goals of mental health become important in any consideration of what the schools should accept as a responsibility to American children. The challenge of helping children acquire sound mental health is too important not to be of concern to the American teacher.

5. Cultural Anthropology and Education

THE MOST SIGNIFICANT ACCOMPLISHMENT of anthropology during the first half of the twentieth century has been the extension and clarification of the concept of culture.[1] Most cultural anthropologists take it for granted that culture is the basic and central concept of their science. Although there is not total agreement among all professionals concerning a precise definition of culture, there is sufficient generic meaning to indicate a considerable need for this science to be included in any total study of the theory and practice of professional education.

Anthropology may be considered the most molar of the social sciences. Conceiving the largest possible units of society as areas of structural-functional study, anthropologists have developed theoretical tools and techniques for describing and analyzing "cultural wholes." These theoretical techniques may have to be enlarged and defined as anthropologists probe to greater depth in the analysis of modern complex cultures. Notwithstanding, the fact remains that culture as culture is the province and speciality of the cultural anthropologists.[2]

When one speaks of anthropology and education, and particularly what the former might contribute to the professionalization and advancement of the latter, there is need for definition and structuralization.

A basic definition of culture, by E. B. Taylor, has generally been accepted for over half a century. Culture was conceived to be that "complex whole which includes knowledge, belief, art, morals, law, custom, and any other capabilities and habits acquired by man as a member of society."[3] Leslie White, in an attempt to develop a more precise definition, has suggested that culture is a class of things and events dependent upon symbolizing. White states that the "locus of

---

[1] A. L. Krober, *The Nature of Culture*, Chicago: University of Chicago Press, 1952, p. 139.

[2] John Gillan, "The Application of Anthropological Knowledge to Modern Mass Society," *Human Organization*, Vol. 15, No. 4, Winter, 1957, p. 29.

[3] *Primitive Culture*, London, 1872.

culture has existence in space and time, (1) within human organisms, *i.e.*, concepts, beliefs, emotions, attitudes; (2) within process of social interaction among human organisms; and (3) within material objects (axes, factories, railroads, pottery bowls) lying outside human organisms but within the patterns of social interaction among them."[4]

The word education has been used in many different ways. From designations of such general character as the totality of influences that both nature and man exercise on our intelligence to a narrow provincial acceptance of mere verbal ability to repeat scriptural doctrine of fundamentalist religions, students and scholars have formulated philosophical and practical definitions of education and the educated man. It would seem advantageous, however, to consider education as directional rather than as many disparate elements which may or may not produce change in men. Émile Durkheim has suggested that from an anthropological and sociological point of view, education must be more meaningful than many modern educational philosophies suggest. Durkheim stated, "Education is the influence exercised by adult generations on those not yet ready for social life. Its object is to arouse and to develop in the child a certain number of physical, intellectual, and moral states which are demanded of him by both the political society as a whole and the special milieu for which he is specifically destined."[5]

Even if we agree generally with Durkheim, it would seem necessary to note that education occurs throughout adult life and that adults can and do learn in both formal and informal situations. Durkheim's statement does show, however, that both anthropologist and educator at least agree that formal schooling should assume responsibility for perpetuating the culture and for directing its positive development.

With these definitional preliminaries, we might then address ourselves to the question: What insights does cultural anthropology afford the educational leader of the mid-twentieth century? Perhaps more specifically, what principles of anthropology have emerged which have import for the administration of educational programs?

This study is not about research orientation into the field of anthropology. Nor is it an exhaustive treatment of what one discipline might provide another in fundamental knowledge. At most, it represents an attempt to review some principles of anthropology which seem to have relevance to the study of education.

---

[4] "The Concept of Culture," *American Anthropologist*, Vol. 61, No. 2, April, 1959, p. 234.

[5] *Education and Sociology*, Glencoe, Illinois: The Free Press, 1956, p. 71.

THE GROWTH OF CULTURE

The history of man from the Stone Age to the present era is a wonderful story of cultural growth.[6] The social inheritance of man might be understood with greater clarity if considered from the eyes of the anthropologist. Indeed, evolution in its multitudinous forms, particularly the technological, social, and political, may be viewed in considerable perspective with anthropological understandings. As a single illustration, one might consider the final work of Ralph Linton, who treated the history of mankind with an emphasis on three basic mutations in the determination of the course of human culture.[7] These were: (1) the use of tools, fire, and language; (2) the discovery of how to raise food and domesticate animals; and (3) the discovery of how to obtain power from heat and how to use the scientific method. Linton suggested that mankind may well undergo a fourth mutation involving the use of atomic energy and the penetration of space before it is fully adjusted to the third phase.

With respect to our own complex society, as well as the primitive, the key to any growth or even the transmission of culture must be an understanding of it. The modern educator, at any level of instruction, cannot afford to neglect knowledge of his total inheritance or the role he plays in building upon it.[8]

THE HISTORY OF EDUCATION

An analysis of the history of education through the eyes of the anthropologist substantiates the fact that educational institutions of the twentieth century are the products of several centuries of cultural growth. The impact of universal education felt in the twentieth century stems from a concept of its possibility during the past century. The culture not only demands its fulfillment in the public schools at the present time, but is now demanding that institutions of higher learning prepare to accept it.

Historically, the individual student sought out the teacher; now the teacher is brought to large numbers of pupils. Over time, teaching became more than tutoring, and the culture demanded teaching skills of greater complexity than parents, tutors, or apprenticeships could handle. Thus, from a primitive pattern affording presents and gifts to

---

[6] Ruth Benedict, "The Growth of Culture," in *Man, Culture and Society*, edited by Harry L. Shapiro, New York: Oxford University Press, 1956, p. 188.

[7] *The Tree of Culture*, New York: Alfred A. Knopf Co., 1955.

[8] George A. Spindler, *The Transmission of American Culture*, Cambridge: Harvard Graduate School of Education Publication, 1957.

a single man, American society has shifted to a pattern of forcing all children and even adults to learn. Moreover, the body politic has made constant efforts to equip schools, train teachers, and effect sanctions to make children and young adults learn.

A survey of educational history supports an anthropological thesis that the realistic adaptation of dominant-status adults to new conditions has been more responsible for the development of universal education than the needs of the children as children.[9] Intelligent cultural patterns may be traced, however, to a series of minor changes suggested to children in school and promoted when these children reach the adult-dominant status.

In historical perspective, but in light of educational objectives, it is possible to trace a reduction in man's inhumanity to man. This problem has not been completely solved, however, but in a projection of the history of education it is possible to contemplate an increase of interpersonal, intercultural, and intersocietal understandings. Certainly, this is a basic need in a world which can be circumnavigated in a matter of hours, and one to which schools should give attention as a means of eliminating prejudice and provincialism.

THE COMPARABILITY OF ALL HUMAN CULTURES

One of the basic emphases of cultural anthropology has been the comparability of all human cultures. This concept has profound implications for education. Although anthropologists have observed that each human culture is unique and embodies a whole way of life for the people within, since World War II there has been greater emphasis upon the "comparability concept." Margaret Mead has summarized an emergent principle:

> Each viable human culture, whether that of a handful of Eskimos or of a nation of fifty million people, must be seen as a system which contains provision for all "normal" human beings who are born within it, with the recognition that, as we make technical and ethical advances, more previously discarded individuals, such as the blind, the deaf, the frail cerebral palsied, will be included within the communication system of the culture.[10]

---

[9] Ralph Linton, "Potential Contributions of Cultural Anthropology to Teacher Education," *Culture and Personality*, Washington, D.C.: American Council of Education, 1941.

[10] Cultural Factors in Community-Education Programs," *Community Education: Principles and Practices from World-Wide Experience*, The Fifty-eighth Yearbook of the National Society for the Study of Education, Chicago: University of Chicago Press, 1959, p. 91.

Studies of cultural comparabilities have also indicated that languages, mores, or any other part of a whole system of a culture developed by one group of human beings can be learned by normal human beings in another group.[11] In fact, anthropologists have concluded that people can be shaped in almost any direction. Questions remain chiefly in the area of "control" and conditioning — how far the direction of cultural growth might be determined by educators or others who presume to teach children or adults.

PATTERN CHANGE

Concomitant with general knowledge acquired by studying the comparability of cultures has been the more specific understandings of "pattern change." The behavior of people is not haphazard, but conforms to a pattern, and parts of the pattern of behavior are interrelated.[12] Anthropologists have concluded that the life of a people may be oriented in many different yet definite directions, and that while value-judgments may not be analyzed with strict scientific validity, values *per se* seem to be a most important subject for objective consideration.

Whereas historically it was assumed that slow educational change was necessary for the welfare of people caught in cultural lag, it is now suggested that rapid change, in which a whole culture is transformed, may be less traumatic than slow, uneven change. Margaret Mead has stated, "Groups, primitive or present, who have a clear, coherent cultural tradition may be able to change their entire way of life in a very few years, carrying the entire community, grandparents, parents, and grandchildren with them, and take on a new life's view in a very few years, provided they are presented with living models of the new culture."[13]

With this possibility, educators find themselves face to face with the question posed by George Counts three decades ago: *Do the Schools Dare Build a New Social Order.*[14] Although Leslie White and other strong advocates of the science of "culturology" or cultural determinism would reject any such possibility, the evidence is not conclusive in their favor.[15] Certainly there is evidence that the culture has con-

---

[11] *Ibid.*

[12] Eugene A. Nida, *Customs and Cultures*, New York: Harper & Brothers, 1954.

[13] Mead, *op. cit.*

[14] New York: The John Day Company, 1932.

[15] Leslie A. White, *The Science of Culture*, New York: Grove Press, 1949.

trolled to a considerable degree the development of educational patterns. In the context of interaction, however, one cannot deny the influence on culture of new ideas or the power of a dynamic personality.

Essentially, if the educator should attempt to change society, the task would be that of teaching different values, even though many values lie beneath the realm of consciousness. And if education can proceed with full recognition that new conditions of life may be met and new patterns of culture emerge through understanding the real importance of how man thinks and feels rather than how be behaves, there may be greater correlation between the objectives of education and the achievement of the pupil.

The anthropologists have not answered the question concerning whether or not the schools should build a new social order. They have not indicated how much educational effort would be needed to change cultural patterns. They have indicated the possibility.

THE VALUE SYSTEM OF A MODERN CULTURE

An analysis of various values and value systems in both primitive and modern societies affords considerable insight in understanding the behavior of people. Thus, the utilization of an "ethos approach" may be most important in studying a community or nation, and ultimately important in developing improved programs of education.

John Gillan has noted that the ethos approach suggests that even complex cultures have a "core" and that once this is understood the other aspects of the culture can, in part at least, be interpreted in terms of it. "The search for a common ethos or basic controlling pattern, or value system of a modern culture, is an attempt to grasp a reliable conception of the culture as a whole while avoiding the methodological difficulties, which are presented by large scale complexity of sub-cultural content and integration, and revolutionary change."[16]

Values are the principles of a culture even though there are usually differences between what is believed and what is said and done. Some anthropologists have noted that the ideals proclaimed by men are in a sense the ultimate value system of a culture.[17] Only by understanding the ideal value system, the emotional intensity man attaches to some values within the system, and the relationship of these

---

[16] "The Application of Anthropological Knowledge to Modern Mass Society," *Human Organization*, Vol. 15, No. 4, Winter, 1957, p. 26.

[17] *See:* Ethel M. Albert, "The Classification of Values," *American Anthropologist*, Vol. 58, No. 2, April, 1956.

values to the behavior of people within the culture, can one fit the culture into a pattern and effect closure.[18] A. L. Kroeber has appraised this aspect of anthropological study.

We can act as if our culturally acquired but preferentially held values were absolute, and, in general that is what we do when we have to act, even if we consider ourselves relativists. We do not review the hundreds of other value systems and paralyze our decision, but we use our own value system, act according to it, and abide by the consequences. As human beings, that is all we can ordinarily do.[19]

Values then may be considered permanent and relative. Education becomes the means whereby values might be recognized for what they are, and educators become the agents of interaction in promoting the acceptance of values which might afford the establishment of a better society in which to live.

COMMUNITY STUDIES AND TECHNIQUES OF THE ANTHROPOLOGIST

The "ethnologizing" of modern national cultures has been a step forward in understanding the behavior of individual man and his group life. Ethnographic studies of subcultures or of single communities within a nation are important for teachers interested in developing insights into the behavior of children. These community studies have indicated that a method of science can be developed in a study of group life.[20] Collection of data is meaningless, of course, without a method of science to determine their value and guide their interpretation. Anthropology has given some direction in this field.[21]

The ethnographic method has at least developed a means of classifying sources according to time, place, and manner in which information is obtained. Ethnographic studies of community life have provided information showing important power structures and informal organizations operating in society. These studies have also been helpful in determining the real *values* held by people in a community.

---

[18] A. L. Kroeber, "Concluding Review," in *An Appraisal of Anthropology Today*, edited by Sol Tax, et al., Chicago: University of Chicago Press, 1953.

[19] *Ibid.*, p. 376.

[20] Ralph Linton, "Potential Contributions of Cultural Anthropology to Teacher Education," *Culture and Personality*, Washington, D.C.: American Council on Education, 1941, p. 15.

[21] W. Lloyd Warner, *Structure of American Life*, Edinburgh: The University Press, 1952.

Anthropologists have developed interviewing techniques as a scientific means of extracting valid information from "real" people. The techniques have been clinical rather than statistical, documentary or of the questionnaire variety. The anthropologist has developed the research technique of participant-observer to a considerable degree of proficiency. Conclusions made through the use of these methods of research may be more valid than many other common techniques used by other social scientists.

CULTURE AND PERSONALITY

No other subject has been afforded more deference and investigation by the psychologist and educator than has that of personality. One can only be impressed with the vast amount of research in both psychology and psychiatry which has promoted a better understanding of the concept, structure, and development of human personality. The anthropologist has related this most molecular of the social sciences, psychology, to the analysis of man's personality as a social being. Personality is an organization which lies behind behavior and within the individual. Values learned in early childhood become persisting forces of personality and help in the determination of responses to various social situations.

The social life of man cannot be observed in totality if separated from societal means and values or from the psychological structuralization of the individual.

Thus, any explanation of culture should involve the psychological level. It is necessary to keep in mind that culture as a social fact is constantly impinging upon the development of the individual personality, while, in turn, the causes of cultural phenomena are personal. Thus, personality, culture, and society form systems of integrated "wholes" having real existence only in consideration of each other. The phenomenon of *interaction* again assumes a position of primary importance.

ANTHROPOLOGY AND HUMAN NATURE

It would seem as if the most important contribution anthropology has made to the study of man, his intellectual and physical development, his culture, and his emotional dispositions, is to be found in the analysis of *human nature*. Indeed, the findings of anthropologists give foundation for the proposition that education can improve society by discarding historical concepts of the innate nature of man. Most of what we have previously called human nature, and upon which culture has been built, is not "nature" at all. Early training and early inculcation of values has been mistaken for human nature. Linton proclaimed, "We have positive proof that most of the values and attitudes which cause trouble in our society cannot be innate since they are lacking in one society or another."[22]

Cutting across both sciences and the humanities, and across the social and behavioral sciences, anthropology substantiates the proposition that human equality is possible and valid.[23] Anthropology has thereby denoted additional responsibility to the role of the educator. Because of the importance of facts in transmitting culture and in suggesting improvement, the interpretation of these facts seems important. Teachers and professors have a great responsibility of assuming the role of "interpreter."

Ashley Montagu has summarized an anthropological view of human nature.

> What anthropology is capable of doing for the student, at all levels of education from the elementary school to the university, is first and foremost to give him an understanding of his own place in the world in relation to the rest of animated nature in all its forms. It is important for the healthy development of the person to be rooted in the great tradition — and all its varieties — of humanity. It is the great understanding of what it means to be human that is the principal contribution that anthropology has to make to the human being of a process of being taught to be human. And learning to be human, and to understand what is involved, should, it seems to me, be the principal purpose of education to which all else is secondary. It is perhaps only when this has been fully recognized that anthropology will assume its proper place at the centrum of all general education.[24]

In a personal reference, Montagu writes with firm belief that no other subject is capable of humanizing the student as is the study of anthropology.

> And by "humanizing" I mean not only enabling the student to feel that nothing that is human is alien to him, but to remain all

---

[22] Linton, *op. cit.*, p. 12.

[23] A. Irving Hallowell, "Culture, Personality, and Society," in *Anthropology Today: An Encyclopedic Inventory*, edited by A. L. Kroeber, Chicago: University of Chicago Press, 1953.

[24] M. F. Ashley Montagu, *Anthropology and Human Nature*, Boston: Porter Sargent Publisher, 1957, pp. 3–7.

his life actively interested in constructively increasing his own and others' understanding of what it means to be human. Today more than ever such understanding has become critically necessary. And I would go so far as to say that of all forms of understanding this will always remain the most adaptively valuable. I know of no other subject which can teach us more helpfully how to understand other societies, or how best to meet their needs.[25]

Undoubtedly, one of the most insidious anachronisms faced by the modern educator has been the faulty interpretation of human nature by many societal groups. Historically, many beliefs about human nature have created "trapped universals" in the minds of men to the extent that the most important species characteristics of man, thinking and high educability, have been thwarted by the time the child enters school. In a vicious circle, man has continued to develop educational programs based upon concepts of human nature suggesting an intrinsic "goodness" or "badness" of himself rather than upon propositions more nearly validated by the sciences.

At first sight, this seems like a hopeless dilemma, for men can teach only what they know, and they have known so little about human nature. Anthropologists' research has indicated that there is an avenue whereby man might find convergence for his many conflicting concepts of his being.

It has been suggested that "anthropology holds up a great mirror to man and lets him look at himself in his infinite variety."[26] In his mirror, man might see that he is indeed unique, reflecting both biological and psychological propensities affording creative expression beyond culture's necessity. In contemplating his variety, man might adopt humility and perspective, building character without external sanction, which will afford him greater opportunity of "means" to greater opportunity of "ends."

---

[25] *Ibid.*
[26] Clyde Kluckholn, *Mirror for Man*, New York: Whittlessey House, 1949.

6. Jurisprudence and Education

EDUCATION OCCUPIES A UNIQUE POSITION in the complex system of American democracy. The relationship of education to jurisprudence has been noted by some students, but seldom discussed in lecture or the literature. Perhaps the diversified training programs for both the attorney and the educator have precluded the study of the philosophy of law in relationship to the unique function of education in this nation.

It has been observed that jurisprudence and education both suffer from too many words with too many meanings. Whereas the general values of education are apparent and acceptable to society at large, the values of understanding specifically the various juristic theories have been mostly academic, and of interest only to the legal profession.

The administration of public education is related directly to law. Indeed, educational administration is founded on law, and is responsible to the people through legal authorities and agencies. If the educational system is to accomplish the task assigned, it seems imperative that educational leaders know and understand the philosophy of law and governmental processes and the historical means of social control.

DIVERGENT THEORIES OF LAW

Concepts of law are as old as "thinking man." The doctrine of natural law is found in the writings of the Greek and Roman Stoics. Essentially, natural law is a "higher law," originally perceived as being promulgated by Deity, but more recently considered as established in "reason."

Natural law rests on the assumption that there is in existence an immutable idea of law which is securely grounded upon a rational order of the cosmos.[1] The nature of man is presumed to remain the same throughout the ages. When Plato tried to define and determine the ideal justice, he spoke in terms of geometry.[2] "Geometrical truth has

---

[1] Edgar Bodenheimer, "Some Recent Trends in European Political Thought," *The Western Political Quarterly*, Vol. 2, 1949, pp. 45–48.

[2] Ernest Cassirer, *The Myth of the State*, New Haven: Yale University Press, 1946.

not been 'made' by anyone; it simply 'is.'"³ The unwritten law, the higher laws, have no beginning in time; they have not been created by man. As the poet observed: "Not of today, nor yesterday, the same throughout all time they live; and whence they came, none knoweth."⁴

In the Middle Ages, Thomas Aquinas accorded a significant and exalted position to natural law. Saint Thomas defined law in a fourfold classification: (1) eternal law, (2) divine law, (3) natural law, and (4) human law.⁵ The first of these, eternal law, was considered almost identical with the reason of God. The second, divine law, was equated to revelation. This concept was dismissed generally, and scarcely considered by later students of the law or church government. The third, natural law, was described as a reflection of divine reason in created things. The inherent inclination of man to live in society, to have children, to educate these children, and to seek truth was implied in natural law. The substance of natural law was thought to be structured in "reason." Promulgated by the Stoics, defined by Cicero, developed by the Christian Fathers, substantiated in logic by Thomas Aquinas, natural law emerged as one of the most important concepts in the philosophical discussions of early Western civilization.

Natural law is not a written law, although man may reduce it to writing. Natural law is an ensemble of things to do and not to do which follow from the fact that man is more than an animal. It is a moral law. Furthermore, four centuries after Thomas Aquinas, the moral foundation of natural law was as acceptable to John Locke as it had been for Saint Thomas. Indeed, for both of these philosophers, man was bound by reason, and the power of church and state was observed as necessary for keeping positive law in agreement with natural law.

Rulers were to be bound by reason, and the attempt to govern was to be based on an agreement between positive and natural law. Sabine noted:

> Enactment is less an act of will than adjustment to the time and circumstance; the granting of dispensations or pardons is a way of meeting cases where the literal interpretations of Human Law would be inequitable, but the ruler's power to do such is only that which is implied in the guardianship of the common good. . . . Above all the rulership of one man over

---

³ Plato, *Republic*, Cornford translation, New York: Oxford University Press, 1945, p. 238.

⁴ Sophocles, *Antigone*, Murray translation, London: George Allen and Unwin, 1941, p. 38.

⁵ Thomas Aquinas, *Summa Theologica*, Pegis translation, Vol. II, Question XCI, Articles 1–5, New York: Random House, 1904, pp. 748–55.

another must not take away the free moral agency of the subject. No man is bound to obedience in all respects, and even the soul of the slave is free.[6]

In the twentieth century, the moral foundation of the natural law concept has not changed. Human happiness is perceived as related to moral virtue. Primitive impulses and irrational appetites must be rectified through education of the ordination of the good life as the ultimate end. Passion must be disciplined and habituated to obedience suggested by reason. An Aristotelian objective of education is still acceptable to many persons. Reason must "be disciplined in the habit of applying knowledge to the affairs of action and emotion, of making choices deliberately and in the light of counsel."[7]

This premium placed upon reason is the essence of education, and education equated to a natural law may be superior to education equated only to human enactments. The right of life is more than the right to exist. The right of life implies also the right to spend it for worthwhile ends achieved through education. And natural law which espouses this concept has received institutional recognition and constitutional embodiment.[8]

Eight years after the famous Bonham Case, John Locke produced his second *Treatise on Civil Government*, in which natural law also was equated to natural rights of the individual. And of these rights, liberty, at least, could not be secure without education. The rights of "life, liberty, and estate" were all important in considering the relationship of man to the state and to society.

Maritain has defined the first rights of man and his relationship to the universe in the twentieth century. The concept of natural law remains important.

> There is, by very virtue of human nature, an order or a definite disposition which human reason can discover and according to which the human will must act in order to attune itself to the necessary ends of the human being. The unwritten law, is nothing more than this.[9]

---

[6] George H. Sabine, *A History of Political Thought*, New York: Henry Holt and Co., 1947, pp. 255–56.

[7] Mortimer J. Adler, *What Man Has Made of Man*, New York: Longmans, Green and Co., 1947, p. 230.

[8] E. S. Corwin, "Debt of American Constitutional Law to Natural Law Concepts," *Notre Dame Lawyer*, Vol. 25, Winter, 1950, pp. 258–84.

[9] Jacques Maritain, *The Rights of Man and Natural Law*, New York: D. C. Anson & Co., 1947, p. 61.

It seems as if Adler has epitomized the thinking of the educator adhering to the natural law concept in the current century.[10] Standing firm against the positivist, he asserted that reason will lead to truth. To argue this thesis, the modern proponents attempt to show that inductively there is established a distinction between knowledge and opinion. Truth is objective and the same for all men because it is an agreement of the mind with reality. There is a difference between sense impression and cognitive knowledge. Further, it can be shown that man knows more things than can be acquired by his senses alone.

Perhaps the greatest contribution to twentieth-century thought on natural law made by Adler and other persons who concur with him has been the attempt to synthesize and note that a certain amount of truth is found in the basic doctrines developed by many historical philosophers.[11] Plato, Aristotle, Saint Thomas, John Locke, Rousseau, Immanuel Kant, and Thomas Jefferson affirmed natural law, even though they differed on many particulars. These philosophers held at least the following principles in common: (1) the positive law made by a state is not the only direction of conduct which applies to many persons living in a society; (2) there are rules or principles of universal application which apply to all men, and not merely to one man or even to one society of a given time or place; (3) there are rules of conduct which are not man-made and which are not positive in the same sense of being posited; (4) man may, through the exercise of reason, discover these universal laws or principles of conduct; (5) these principles are the general source of all particular rules of conduct, even those which individuals make for themselves or governments make and seek to maintain by force; and (6) these principles constitute the standard by which all other rules are to be judged good or bad, right or wrong, just or unjust.[12]

Essentially natural law asserts that there is, by the very virtue of human nature and the very order of the cosmos, a relationship which human reason can discover and to which men must react in order to attain the necessary ends of human existence.

Opposed to the concept of natural law is the deterministic or imperative theory. This theory denies at the outset an everlasting idea of law and an absolute knowledge of truth, and maintains that there is

---

[10] Mortimer J. Adler, *A Dialectic of Morals*, New York: Harcourt, Brace and Company, 1941.

[11] Harold Gill Reuschlin, *Jurisprudence — Its American Prophets*, Indianapolis: The Bobbs-Merrill Co., 1951.

[12] Bodenheimer, *op. cit.*

only a postive law. Positive law is not based on innate ideas and self-evident precepts of reason. Positive law is mostly a reflection of material, social, and economic relationships, and may be perceived as necessary in order to control the irrational behavior of man.

The attempt to separate law from ethics and morals is traced to Machiavelli and Thomas Hobbes. Not until John Austin in the nineteenth century, however, was a definitive philosophy of analytical jurisprudence established which proposed that positive law was divorced from both theological origins and the metaphysics of idealism. Austin wrote, "Positive law is set, directly or circuitously, by a sovereign individual or body, to a member or members of the independent political society wherein its author is supreme."[13] In other words, Austin was declaring that the citizens of a sovereign political state were subject to the statutes and laws established by those in control of the state. It remained for Hans Kelsen in the twentieth century to promulgate a "pure theory of law."[14]

Analytical jurisprudence asserts that law is a command which is written down for the guidance of the intelligent persons and has power over these persons by virtue of a sanction potentially available.[15] Ultimately, positive law was divorced from morals, but not necessarily from ethics. The concept of positive law led legislatures, monarchs, and courts to acclaim that the words "be it enacted" justified whatever followed.[16] The fundamental reality of positive law is observed in the organized force and power of the state. Law is a technique of social control. Coercion is an essential element of positive law.

Hans Kelsen has written:

> The Pure Theory of Law restricts itself to a structural analysis of positive law based on a comparative study of the social orders which actually exist and existed in history under the name of law. . . . The pure theory of law deals with the law as a system of valid norms created by acts of human beings.[17]

---

[13] John Austin, *Jurisprudence: The Philosophy of Positive Law*, Vol. I, London: John Murray Co., 1879, p. 339.

[14] Hans Kelsen, *General Theory of Law and State*, translated by Anders Wedberg, Cambridge: Harvard University Press, 1945.

[15] Albert Kocourk, "The Century of Analytical Jurisprudence," *Law — A Century of Progress*, Vol. II, New York: New York University Press, 1937.

[16] Roscoe Pound, "Fifty Years of Jurisprudence," *Harvard Law Review*, Vol. 51, 1938, pp. 445–46.

[17] Hans Kelsen, "Law, State and Justice," *Yale Law Journal*, Vol. 57, January, 1948, p. 382.

He had written previously that:

> It is commonplace that law and morals (in the broader sense of the term) are not identical; that there is moral as well as immoral law; that men may be obliged in law to do something forbidden by ethics. This independence of the law and morals is expressed in the phrase "positive law." This phrase, which has many meanings, means in this connection that law, more or less arbitrarily created, has value only for a determined epoch, at a determined place, for a determined group of men, *i.e.*, that law has only a relative value, whereas morals — especially if of a religious nature, revealed as the will of Deity — represents an absolute value. . . . If there were a social order, absolutely good, following from nature, from reason, or from divine will, the activity of the legislator would be the idle attempt of artificial lighting in full sunshine. And the usual objection: that there is justice, but it cannot be or — what amounts to the same — it cannot be unequivocally determined is a contradiction in terms, a contradition serving as a typically ideological veil of the truth, and, alas, too painful fact. Justice is an irrational ideal. It may be indispensable for the will and actions of men, but it is inaccessible to cognition. Cognition can only deal with positive law.[18]

E. W. Patterson has summarized the contributions of the pure theory of law in the development of modern jurisprudence.[19] First, it is a concept of law which may separate theory from practice. "Kelsen's theory asserts that a legal norm (rule or principle, judicial or legislative in origin) may be valid law despite its incompatibility with some extraneous norm." Second, the pure theory of law provides a concept of law which includes the case law of judicial and administrative tribunals as well as the norms set down by the legislature. Thus, there is acknowledgment of power norms and decisional norms. Third, the theory of pure law posits a dynamic legal order rather than a static one. Orderliness is stressed as an immediate end, but not as a geometric order which is complete and absolute. Fourth, the question, "Do courts make law?" is answered in the affirmative. "Every act of law-applying is also an act of law-creating." In contradistinction to the legal interpretations of the nineteenth century, the courts do not merely find the law, they create it. Finally, it is said that Kelsen's conception

---

[18] Hans Kelsen, "The Pure Theory of Law," in *Law — A Century of Progress*, New York: New York University Press, 1937, pp. 234–36.

[19] E. W. Patterson, "Hans Kelsen and His Pure Theory of Law," *California Law Review*, Vol. 40, 1952.

of law serves to resolve an ancient jurisprudence paradox. The law must provide stability, but it cannot stagnate and remain the same. It must develop and progress with the times. The theory of pure law has made a contribution toward relieving tension between philosophical aspects of "being" and "becoming" in law. "The stability of law does not consist merely in the rules and principles which prescribe law conduct and are guides to judicial and administrative decisions, but are also in the power of officials to change the law."[20]

It must not be assumed that only two theories of law exist. There are as many divergent and developmental concepts of law as of men who philosophize about them. The various jurisprudence concepts indicate consideration of the great philosophical questions of man in history. The realists[21] and pragmatists[22] are as insistent in their jurisprudence as in their analysis of epistemology and education *per se*. The neo-Kantian, neo-Hegelian, and French jurists have all contributed significant ideas in juristic philosophy.[23] From the philosophy of Roscoe Pound[24] to the constitutionalism of E. S. Corwin,[25] divergent concepts of law have emerged. These philosophies have attempted to bridge the gap between the two extremes, and have provided considerable speculation on the "real nature of law."

One thing, at least, remains clear and consistent. In the modern

---

[20] *Ibid.*, p. 9.

[21] *See:* Karl N. Llewellyn, *Jurisprudence: Realism in Theory and Practice*, Chicago: University of Chicago Press, 1962.

[22] *See:* Thomas A. Cowan, "Legal Pragmatism and Beyond," in *Interpretation of Modern Legal Philosophies*, edited by Paul Sayre, New York: Oxford University Press, 1947, pp. 132–42.

[23] Gustave Radbruch's philosophy of law is based on a neo-Kantian concept of values. Justice is an essential component of law. There must also be a moral and/or purpose of law. Without justice and moral purpose, true law is nonexistent. "Legal positivism has been unable out of its own resources to construct any justification or explanation for the obligatory force of law. Adherents of the positivistic philosophy believe they can prove the obligatory force of law simply by showing that it is backed by a power sufficient to enforce it. But though compulsion can be based on power, the obligatory quality of law cannot be. This must be founded rather on a value that inheres in law without reference to its content. It is always better than no rule of law at all in the sense it at least creates legal security and certainty." *See:* Josef Kohler, *Philosophy of Law*, translated by Albrecht, New York: The MacMillan Co., 1914. Quoted in L. E. Fuller, "American Legal Philosophy at Mid-Century, "*Journal of Legal Education*, Vol. 6, 1954, pp. 457–85.

[24] Roscoe Pound, "Scope and Purpose of Sociological Jurisprudence," *Harvard Law Review*, Vol. 25, 1912.

[25] Edward S. Gorwin, "The Higher Background of American Constitutional Law," *Harvard Law Review*, Vol. 42, 1928.

era, law must be based on something more than naked power and/or authority. Acts of authority are not always considered justified, and consequently may not be obeyed if they are simply arbitrary and impulsive dictates of power. Law must be considered as a relationship between God and man, man and man, or the state and man, which relationship might be enforced by some type of authority. It would seem as if the consciousness of humanity must be related to the rules which govern the external conduct of man. Perhaps, therefore, categorical injunctions must indicate purpose as well as potential sanction in the attempted control of particular individual wills and society at large.

The formula might be found in positive law declaring principles of the natural law. Indeed, rules of positive law might be written as specific statements of natural justice. These principles or rules may direct the affairs of a particular community in a manner befitting the current circumstances of its historical character.[26] There might be positive law, which somehow tends to become an embodiment of natural justice, but generally there is a difference between natural and positive law.

Adler has written extensively on the difference between these two concepts of law. He insists that no definition can ever embody both natural and positive law since they are not of the same essence. Positive law compels obedience by an exertion of external force; natural law does not. Positive law is promulgated by legislation or command, whereas natural law is discovered by natural inquiry. Positive law obligates only those persons within a community wherein it is instituted. Natural law conceives of absoluteness, and cannot accept relativity or specificity in legal relationships which should exist among men or between man and the state. Natural law is the *principle* of law; positive law is a rule, or at most a precept.[27]

EDUCATIONAL ADMINISTRATION AND THE PHILOSOPHY OF LAW

The administration of the public services has had little quarrel with the various and diverse conceptual developments of positive law.

---

[26] Mortimer J. Adler, *How to Think About War and Peace*, New York: Simon and Schuster, 1944.

[27] Mortimer J. Adler, "The Doctrine of Natural Law in Philosophy," *University of Notre Dame Law Proceedings*, Vol. 67, 1947.

Administration *per se* is not inconsistent with any form or theory of law, providing the intent of the legislation or mandate is known. The creation of governmental agencies to effect the law is both legal and proper. The educational administrator is a professional employee, and by virtue of his office he executes and administers the policies of a superordinate authority.

In fulfilling the responsibilities and obligations inherent in this office, the administrator is also in a position to make law as the need arises. This law may be called "Rules and Regulations," but it has the effect of law if it can be enforced. When philosophical questions are posed about education, however, theories of positive law may not always apply. Why should all persons be afforded an education? What kinds of education should be made available? What are the ultimate objectives of education? These are questions which disturb educators who organize and administer programs based solely on enactments of positive law.

Most modern theories of education may well support the proposition that the positive law formulated for the control of society should reflect natural-law principles. Generally, the American public school educator has minimized the importance of law in relationship to aims of education. Indeed, according to many educational administrators, the position of education in the American nation is unique, and may be above and beyond the general concept of positive law. This has been called a basic assumption of educational administration.[28]

THE UNIQUE STATUS OF EDUCATION

The principle "seek the good" directs man to an end which is happiness or the possession of what is good for man as man.[29] The principle "seek an education" is a step in the direction of obtaining what is good for man. The necessity of conforming to popular impulses, as expressed through the executive and legislative branches of government, may severely hamper the fulfillment of man's highest educational destiny. In such a case, education occupies a unique place in the institutional structure of the American nation, and may rightly propose programs and direction which might transcend positive law enactments.

---

[28]*See:* F. Robert Paulsen, "Basic Assumptions of Educational Administration," *Peabody Journal of Education*, Vol. 34, March, 1957, pp. 270–83.

[29]Howard R. McKinnon, "Natural Law and Positive Law," *Notre Dame Lawyer*, Vol. 13, January, 1948, pp. 125–39.

Indeed, such has been the position of education since the time of Socrates. If the word truth might replace the word God in the Platonic Dialogue, education assumes a unique position. Socrates, on trial for his life, argued that education, or the search for truth, transcended the positive law.

> Men of Athens, I honor you, but I shall obey God rather than you, and while I have life and strength, I shall never cease from the practice and teachings of philosophy, exhorting anyone whom I meet after my manner, and convincing him, saying: Oh my friend, why do you who are a citizen of the great and mighty and wise city of Athens care so much about laying up the greatest amount of money and honor and reputation, and so little about the wisdom and truth and the greatest improvement of the soul, which you never regard or heed at all? Are you not ashamed of this? And if the person with whom I am arguing says: Yes, but I do care; I do not depart or let him go at once; I interrogate and examine and cross-examine him, and if I think that he has no virtue, but only says that he has, I reproach him with undervaluing the greater, and overvaluing the less. And this I should say to everyone whom I meet, young and old, citizen and alien, but especially to the citizens, inasmuch as they are my brethren. For this is the command of God, as I would have you know, and I believe that to this day no greater good has ever happened in the State than my service to the God. For I do nothing but to go about persuading you all, old and young alike, not to take thought for your persons and your properties, but first and chiefly to take care about the greatest improvement of the soul.[30]

Assuredly, sincerity of conviction or faith in an abstract concept are not reliable tests of truth. But this argument does not deny the existence of a law more applicable to the service of education in many instances than the mere enactment of positive law. If the traditional, classical theory of natural law is not acceptable to modern scholars who reject the Stoic, Christian, or rational origins of the concept, perhaps there is another premise for consideration. Many educators have suggested a concept of natural law that actually avoids the juristic paradoxes of the classical theory and recognizes that men naturally differ widely in abilities and experiences. Men differ in their intepretation of the phenomena of the universe and of life itself. Men differ in

---

[30] Plato, "Apology," in *Man and Man: The Social Philosophers*, edited by Saxe Commins and Robert N. Linscott, New York: Random House, 1947, pp. 198–99.

their emotional, physical, and mental reactions to stimuli, and in their ability to work with abstractions and conceptual information.

At least one theory of natural law has been proposed which takes the differences of humanity into account.

> There is a wide variety in man's power of imagination in the sensitivity to beauty, poetry, art and music, in his attitudes toward love, sympathy, sacrifice, charity, and honor, and in his responses to religious rituals. These capacities and attitudes change from time to time, from nation to nation, from group to group, from family to family, and from man to man. Man is not like the robin, the same now as always, the same here as elsewhere, one individual like every other individual. It is contrary to his nature to have uniformity in aptitude, in preference, in feeling, in taste, in attitude toward his fellows. By nature his thought does not conform to any given standard. Is it not then in accordance with the *law of nature* that men differing in background, tradition, experience, taste, and aptitude should also differ in ideas, judgments, ideals, and faiths?
>
> The natural law which seems deducible from the diversified nature of man is that men *ought* to recognize and accept as natural differences in other men and not forcibly try to eradicate them because they are incompatible with his own beliefs of one another, rather than the acceptance of the absoluteness of any one belief as the key to truth, the way to peace, and the preservation of civilization.
>
> Natural law then, by this view, consists of those rules, which according to the totality of experience of mankind, at any given time and place seem most conductive to its greatness and goodness. . . . By this type of philosophy, man accepts those moral values that have stood the test of time and experience and uses them as the foundation upon which, by his own efforts, to build toward a higher destiny.[31]

Thus, even for the relativist, the pragmatist, and the "progressive," a concept of natural law may be conceived as especially existing on a higher plane than positive law enactments. This concept of natural law would not posit that human life, in specific detail, is the everconstant concern of a cosmic power. It recognizes rather the natural capabilities and inabilities of man. And education, as the acquisition of the spiritual and cultural possessions of humanity, might still transcend ordinary enactments of positive law, contrary to the reason

---

[31] George W. Goble, "Nature, Man and the Law," *American Bar Association Journal*, Vol. 41, May, 1955, pp. 403–407.

inherent in the basic natural law concept or the historical experience of mankind.

The objectives of positive law are governance and control. The objective of education is to enlarge and enrich the lives of individual persons, and yet, it must be admitted that formal education is but one of many interests that make up the lives of human beings. Education is one thing when viewed as a purpose or activity of the state; it is another thing when observed in terms of individual and group behavior.[32]

Thus, considering individual differences and a concept of natural law which accepts them as fact, what are the responsibilities for educating all the children of all the people? Should education be equated to scholarly intellectual achievement? Should good citizenship and an indoctrination of democratic ideals remain the general "practical" goals of American education? The noted philosopher, William Hocking, has written to these points:

> Citizenship is a universal responsibility — all men must qualify; scholarship is not. Scholarship has its special demands which not all fulfill, nor ought to fulfill, nor care to fulfill.
>
> The truth is that in a strict sense of a "right" *there is and can be no such thing as a "right" to education.*
>
> For there can be no education, not even the most elementary, without the living response and cooperation of the subject. No person and no community can unilaterally give anyone "an education." When education is conceived as a commodity, to be claimed at the hands of a benevolent and endlessly resourceful community, to be handed over and passively received, the very sense of education is outraged and degraded.
>
> There is a human right in the education field, a right universal and fundamental, addressed to the society into which one is born. It is the right to such available opportunities, equipments, aids, and open doors as one's own mental demand qualifies him to use, and drives him to take the trouble of using.[33]

Any inconsistency in the thinking of professional educators relative to the position of education in the social matrix may well center in diverse concepts of education as well as of law. When education is viewed solely as a purpose or activity of the state, the relationship to law and administration assumes a definite position. Essentially,

---

[32]*See:* Jesse Sears, "Reason, Propaganda, and Attacks Upon the Schools," *Educational Administration and Supervision*, Vol. 39, January, 1953.

[33] William Hocking, *Experiment in Education*, New York: Henry Regnery & Co., 1954, pp. 272–74.

administration is the execution of positive law, and this execution presumes the power to command. Perhaps within the confines of structure of government, the educational administrator finds it expedient to execute the public law as it applies to education. But if the declaration of positive law appears contrary to a higher law, the administrator — educator, first and foremost — might acknowledge the latter in the attempt to execute the service of his profession rather than concern himself with the specific function of his office as administrator.

Representatives of the legal profession and experts in the political science fields have concurred with the statement that education is a unique service and may transcend positive law if the occasion requires. Faith in public education rests ultimately on the belief that a particular kind of education may be designed to support and promote a specific way of life. It is believed by most educational leaders that free public education will best support and maintain the American way of life.[34]

Charles A. Beard, foremost American political scientist and historian, drafted a classic statement which was adopted generally by the Educational Policies Commission respecting the unique function of education in American democracy.

> Disturbing events bring forcibly to the foreground the necessity for assuring to educational authorities throughout the entire school system a wide range of freedom in the determination of policies and the conduct of the schools. They are not entitled to, and do not seek, a position of impregnable irresponsibility against society or its matured judgments. They do not deny the validity of the claim that community budgets must be balanced, by curtailments if necessary, in time of stress. They accept the broad principle of democratic control. It is against the ravages of transitory politicians engaged in mere inquisitorial expeditions that they demand protection. They object to having teaching positions in schools and universities turned into the spoils of office, with continuous unsettlements and turnovers from election to election. They protest against allowing any legislative or administrative authority, chosen for other purposes and mainly engrossed in other business, to intervene at will in educational administration, to threaten college presidents, superintendents, and teachers with reprisals, to upset carefully arranged curricula for petty reasons, to dictate the purchase of books and materials, to locate school buildings with respect to real estate projects, and

---

[34] Educational Policies Commission, *The Structure and Administration of Education in American Democracy*, Washington, D.C.: National Education Association, 1938, p. 128.

otherwise to subject the schools to passing tempers and demands of private interests. In stating their position, school authorities merely say that those responsible for educational policies and administration should be in fact responsible, should have powers commensurate with their duties, and should be immune against sporadic raids by men who are not responsible. In so contending they simply assert a fundamental principle of democracy and sound administration. As a unique form of public service, having obligations different from and transcending other services, education must insist upon measures of law designed to assure it that form of autonomy in which it can best discharge its particular functions.[35]

Public education is basic to the permanent and continued existence of our form of government and the freedom it guarantees. The public schools have been charged with the responsibility of transmitting from generation to generation the vast accumulation of knowledge.

The psychologists may develop all types of scientific achievement tests to measure thousands of items on the most minute scale. Community leaders may determine the content of education to serve as propaganda for conditioning the citizen to accepted patterns of political and social life. But the real purpose of education would still be neglected. Ultimately, the purpose of education will remain as a means to develop human beings who can live adequately with their fellow men, and at the same time achieve the highest plane of individual character potential.

Literature and experience have suggested that men are capable of governing themselves and of managing their own affairs. Individuals may be trusted to achieve their own destinies. Democratic government must rest on the assumption that citizens will be informed on matters of public policy, and that citizens will also help formulate that policy. Within democratic or republican governments, men are accorded political freedom inasmuch as they all have enough good will toward one another and enough loyalty to the commonwealth to compromise their differences without resorting to brute force. Reason might always stand as a foundation for justice, tolerance, and fair dealing among men; debate, deliberation, and compromise are supporting means. Education will complement the foundation and secure its mooring.

---

[35] Educational Policies Commission, *The Unique Function of Education in American Democracy*, Washington, D.C.: National Education Association, 1937, pp. 125–26.

Intellectual freedom must remain a paramount consideration for the individual. "Tyranny over the mind of man is tyranny at its worst." If democracy is to be more than a dream, more than a philosophical idea, the highways of human experience must remain clear of deterrent signs and created barriers. Man must develop a tolerance for his fellow man heretofore not observed in human history. Man cannot be intellectually free without having tolerance toward his neighbor's opinions and sentiments. The right to seek truth, to form personal opinions and convictions, and to propagate one's conception of truth must remain a condition of freedom. Man should be able freely to formulate his own value system as long as it does not conflict with the rights of other persons. These are rights afforded to an enlightened people through an education transcending the limitations of positive law based only upon power and force.

Man is a social animal, and by his nature has capacity and need to associate in fraternity. Democracy is a far more complex organization than the form or structure of government. A schematic of the ideal universe does not guarantee any form of philosophy of government. A vision of the actual living of life, a knowledge of human achievement and sufferings, and a recognition of humane control of man's activity represent democratic objectives. It is an assumption of democracy that man is capable of achieving a humaneness, dignity, and worth which command respect from his neighbors. And the ability to achieve is inherent in the nature of man. With this ability, mankind might achieve a governmental structure which promotes individual and social aspirations. Democracy is more than a form of government: it is found in the substance of intelligent cooperation. This cooperation is dependent upon education.[36]

A democratic society will not endure if men insist on pursuing selfish and personal ends. The public interest as well as individual attainment must both remain foremost. Liberty, freedom, and "rights" inescapably have correlative duties and responsibilities. It is an assumption of democracy that citizens will accept these responsibilities required by the general welfare. If necessary, men will unite in restricting the freedom of individual action by legal enactment, sanctioned in force by the collective power of society. Positive law has developed, therefore, and indeed is a paramount instrument in the control of any action of individuals or groups within society. Positive law and government *per se*, as the organized instruments of social control, should

---

[36]John Dewey, *Democracy and Education*, New York: The MacMillan Co., 1916.

indicate power and authority commensurate with the responsibility afforded through the common consent of the people. But less government and less control are needed in proportion to the level of education attained by man, which education should eventually temper gross action through increased understanding of the "self" and of the commonwealth.

In a democracy, the cultural gains and achievements do not accrue to one man alone. Historically, many aspects of cultural progress have belonged to only a few persons. It is an assumption of American democracy that the labor of mankind will not be exploited by a favored few, but rather that all men will share in the heritage and in the future of spiritual and material accomplishments.[37] Democracy postulates the ideal of the equal chance. It survives on the realization of that ideal.

Educational philosophy in the American nation is based on doctrines which oppose theories of divine right and traditional absolutism. These doctrines on which American educational philosophy is based postulate natural rights of man which may transcend the positive law.[38] In affording education a unique position in the fabric of our society and institutional life, America might achieve a destiny heretofore considered only a dream. Democracy calls for a militant faith in education founded upon a concept of natural law allowing the freedom to learn, applicable to the times, and developed through the resourcefulness and energy of the human race.

SUMMARY

Educational leaders in the United States have indicated considerable cognizance of the natural law principles inherent in the national ideology. They have also shown respect for positive law enactments promulgated by the state. There is evidence to show that in this nation there has been some conflict between these two rather fundamental concepts of law. Educational administrators have understood their responsibilities for executing the public law and policies relating to educational development. They have also been concerned with the mission and purpose of education which afforded prospects for individual achievement as well as for the maintenance of the society.

---

[37] *See:* Newton Edwards and Herman G. Richey, *The School in American Social Order*, New York: Houghton Mifflin Co., 1947, pp. 842–43.

[38] Charles E. Merriam, *What is Democracy?* Chicago: University of Chicago Press, 1941.

Collectively, the strength and excellence of individuals become the strength and destiny of the nation. Governments cannot legislate the kinds of education or the standards of achievement possible for individuals to acquire. Governments can provide guidelines respecting minimal standards, but essentially education must and will remain a matter of concern to the individual.

Those who began our national existence held a conviction that there are some aspects of the individual's life which are beyond the control and reach of government. Eminent jurists have noted that the freedom and liberty we enjoy are not possible solely because of our constitutions and laws. Judge Learned Hand said:

> I often wonder whether we do not rest our hopes [for the survival of liberty] too much upon constitutions, upon laws, and upon courts. These are false hopes; believe me, these are false hopes. Liberty lies in the hearts of men and women, when it dies there, no constitution, no law, nor court can ever do much to save it.[39]

Postive law must not be considered the manifestation of some omnipotent power. It should be assumed that the inadequacies of positive law might be eliminated through education.

Historically, the doctrine of natural law has been used to support two distinctly different political theories. Natural law supports the proposition of natural rights developed by John Locke and Thomas Jefferson. Such a concept of law became the basis of our American democracy. The development of such a law suggests the possibility of rule by the people or by their representatives under a government of laws and not of men.

It should be understood, however, that natural law has also been used to support the authoritarianism of various churches or in the supposed creation of an "ideal" state through the exercise of personal power and authority.

The question whether natural law exists may not be important. The more important issue may be in the determination of justice for all persons living under a government of laws. The interpretation of law is extremely important. The process and principles of judicial review in the United States and the premium placed upon education and the enlightened citizenry have been important considerations in the interpretation of natural law.

---

[39] Learned Hand, *Spirit of Liberty*, New York: Alfred A. Knopf Co., 1952, p. 190.

Certainly if statutory law conflicts with goals of the American culture or inhibits the interactive process whereby man learns about himself and his environment, the professional educator is concerned with ways and means by which such laws might be abrogated and/or transcended. There must be respect for the law, but there must also be ways and means available to change the law if it does not serve the purpose of man within the society.

Natural law which posits the intrinsic goodness or badness of man cannot be validated by the sciences today. Human reason finds it difficult to accept such positions. The interaction of man with his culture continues to be important in the final determination and finding of truth. Thus, the interpretation of natural law must remain flexible and capable of incorporating new findings and understandings. Ultimately, however, it does seem likely that the experience of mankind has suggested the validity of certain rules and certain principles which appear natural in consideration of self-achievement and individual destiny.

The Ordinance of 1787, which provided for the government of the Northwest Territory, antedating the Constitution and establishing principles of American democracy, contains the following statement: "Religion, morality, and knowledge being necessary to good government and the happiness of mankind, schools and the means of education shall be forever encouraged." The *Declaration of Independence* transcended the provisions of positive law in acclaiming as a natural right of all mankind the privilege of "*deriving* just powers from the consent of the governed." Certainly, those who believe in and advocate the philosophy of the *Declaration of Independence* maintain that certain rights are inherent in the people. Within the matrix of American jurisprudence, educators submit as a goal of their practice the guarantee of this philosophy.

7. *Education and Man's Search For Self*

IN J. D. SALINGER'S BOOK, *The Catcher in the Rye*,[1] the boy Holden Caulfield philosophizes about the "phony world," "phony people," and his own personal attempt to find meaning in his existence. As the reader sits back to reflect on the conditions which give rise to such a tale, he is disturbed as to why a sixteen-year-old boy should be so overwhelmed by the apparent perplexities and circumstances of life. Holden Caulfield wants desperately to find himself. His insights and interpretations of fact and of life itself are not always correct, but at times he is a rather acute observer of the realities of society. He hates the "phony world," and the world seems to be peopled with many phony characters. He is lost in a labyrinth of contradictions. The inconsistencies of life and the lack of character, as he perceives them, finally drive him beyond sanity.

Much is written about American society today — its ills are listed, described, and analyzed. Sooner or later, some suggest, the panacea for all its problems must be found in education. Education has thus become a religion of the twentieth century. Yet if faith in it is to be warranted, there must be more than preachments and listed objectives — there must be evidence that the "good life" is attainable for all.

Institutional education in the United States has never charted the direction of society. Generally, it has reflected the culture of which it is a part. In fact school curricula seldom, if ever, even keep pace with the culture, let alone posit the direction of cultural change. Education has seldom dealt effectively with the burning problems of America or of world culture.

Because of the many problems confronting American education and American society today, a real marriage of the social and public professions seems necessary. No profession has a monopoly on the concern for individual achievement or the teaching of moral responsibility, nor can any one of them solve, separately, the educational and social problems which face us. More teamwork among professional educators, public health nurses, psychologists, psychiatrists, and social

---

[1] New York: The New American Library, 1962, pp. 184–85.

workers is required. There is need for concerted action and constructive programming among all professional persons interested in the conditions arising from the demands of a fast-moving society.

Annually, we give some evidence of being more willing to spend money to place a man on the moon than to attain all the lofty philosophical and educational goals deemed important for all the people. The schools cannot be expected to respond adequately to all the demands now placed upon them without more help and more support. Teachers, counselors, psychologists, and social workers cannot solve all the problems of the individual and of the family without additional financial support and without relating their work to the demands of formal education.

The financing of these public services, however, should not be the responsibility of the professionals. The financial support of public education, of all public social services, must remain the responsibility of the families, the communities, indeed of society at large. Professionals should not shirk their responsibilities and fail to provide whatever services are possible with whatever support is given. But perhaps professionals must use the Rogerian counseling technique with the adult-dominant-status groups in our society, helping these groups to understand that support is vital if existing problems are to be solved.

OBJECTIVES OF EDUCATION

What are the objectives of education in the public school system in the United States today? One recalls the "Seven Cardinal Aims of Education" written in 1918,[2] "The Purposes of Education in American Democracy" promulgated in 1938,[3] and the "Ten Imperative Needs of Youth" adopted in 1951.[4] Essentially, educators and the public have always agreed that the basic responsibility of the schools is to develop the mind. But they also agree that the overall mission of the schools has been enlarged. Schools are now asked to help each child become as good and as capable in every way as native endowment permits, to help children acquire any skill or characteristic which the community deems worthwhile.[5]

---

[2] Commission on the Reorganization of Secondary Education, *Bulletin No. 35*, Washington, D.C.: U.S. Bureau of Education, 1918, p. 19.

[3] Washington, D.C.: National Education Association, 1938.

[4] *Planning for American Youth*, Washington, D.C.: National Association of Secondary School Principals, 1951.

[5] *The Committee for the White House Conference on Education*, A Report to the President, Washington, D.C.: U.S. Government Printing Office, April, 1956, p. 9.

The order given to the public schools seems simple, and yet grand in its simplicity. In addition to intellectual achievement, the schools are asked to foster morality, show the road to happiness, and teach any useful ability. The talent of each child is to be sought out and developed to the fullest. Each weakness is to be studied and, so far as possible, corrected. This is truly a majestic ideal, and historically a new one. Schools furnishing this kind of instruction have never been provided for more than a small fraction of mankind.[6]

Presumably these objectives are to be universal, and it is this concept of universality that poses a new problem. For there are too many children and too many adults who cannot profit from a lock-step institutional scheme of education organized for an "average" child in some general period of normalcy. Too many persons are unable to find self-realization and social fulfillment within the limitations imposed and the demands required by contemporary society.

In *Children Who Hate*, Fritz Redl and David Wineman discuss case histories of American youth associated with Pioneer House in Michigan.[7] Designed as a laboratory and clinic for children with social problems, this school attempted to determine what causes problems and to provide treatment and education for the children "enrolled." Redl and Wineman indicate that these children were so pessimistic about what the world held for them that an observer, after one glimpse into their lives, could only come away feeling horror that children should live through the things they mentioned. In the words of the authors, "It was amazing that even more destruction of their personalities had not taken place when one reviews the background of these children."[8]

The study suggested that the primary factors which might have created the personalities of these "problem" children were the "missing links" in their lives. What were these missing links?

1. Factors leading to identification with adults; feelings of being loved and wanted; and encouragement to accept values and standards of the adult world.

2. Opportunities for help in achieving a gratifying recreational pattern.

---

[6]*Ibid.*

[7]Glencoe, Ill.: The Fress Press, 1951. Pioneer House developed from the Detroit Group Project founded in 1942 by Fritz Redl as an "agency to serve other agencies" interested in helping "problem" children. It was financed by the Council of Social Agencies of Metropolitan Detroit, and co-sponsored by the School of Social Work, Wayne State University.

[8]*Ibid.*, p. 57.

3. Opportunities for adequate peer relationships.

4. Opportunities for making community ties, establishing a feeling of being "rooted somewhere where one belongs, where other people besides your parents know you and like you."

5. Ongoing family structures which were not in some phase of basic disintegration at almost any given time in their lives.

6. Adequate economic security for some of the basic needs of life.[9]

Observe how many of these responsibilities and opportunities are assumed to be functions of the school today, and yet how many of them have been historically assumed to be functions of the family and of the community!

Not that the picture is altogether dismal with respect to the problems confronting American society or our youth. Society offers much that is wonderful, and the many achievements of a majority of our youth can make us justifiably happy and proud. The writer is merely suggesting that information is available which might prompt the educator — or any reflective person — to question seriously the tasks society now demands of the public schools.

TASKS FOR PROFESSIONAL PERSONNEL

For several decades, those working in the public schools have recognized many of the problems inherent in promoting universal education. We have accepted and preach the doctrine of individual differences. We attempt to develop "special education" programs for the underprivileged and the mentally retarded child. We encourage the gifted child. And now we are told that a great segment of our school population is socially disadvantaged and must be researched and motivated.

Statistics are seldom interesting in a brief treatment of a subject. Nevertheless, some rather well-documented facts have implications for the development of educational programs for America. They would suggest that there are limitations to achievement as well as potentialities for success within the general population.

The number of children receiving assistance under the Aid to Families with Dependent Children program increased from 1.7 million in 1950 to 2.8 million in 1961. This trend suggests that real financial security is not being afforded many of the children in this nation.

The number of illegimate births increased markedly from 142,-000 in 1952 to 209,000 in 1958. A continuation of past increases

---

[9]*Ibid.*

would indicate almost 300,000 illegitimate births in 1970. We are thus faced with problems of the broken home even before the home is established, for thousands of these children.

Juvenile court delinquency cases increased from 280,000 in 1950 to 773,000 in 1959. Does this trend not suggest that society is failing to correct the causes of delinquency and only becoming more involved with the results?

Based on a continuing sample of civilian population taken by the United States National Health Survey, in 1965 there were 1,314,000 persons suffering from mental and nervous disorders. This number has continued to increase. In 1960, over 600,000 persons were hospitalized because of mental disorders, and it is estimated that over one-half the patients hospitalized in the almost 1,800,000 hospital beds in America today may require such hospitalization because of mental and/or psychosomatic illness.[10]

Each of these statistics represents more than one case for both the educator and the social worker. Obviously, educational achievement and social productivity cannot be realized by other members of a family in which delinquency or illness exists. Professionals in all fields, then, should and must assume more responsibility for developing the kind of society in which educational achievement and social productivity are available freely to all.

The tragedy of our time, however, is not the failure of educators to know about the "social dynamite" in our communities. The real tragedy is that powerful community leaders fail to allow persons in public services the opportunities to do much about solving those problems which exist and can be anticipated. At times the educator is forced to play the ostrich because our community "fathers" fail to admit that problems do exist. Yet most people still agree that the schools should provide universal education, with all its lofty objectives, for all American children.

In most communities educators cannot presently do much beyond what the politicians, statesmen, business executives, and other community leaders allow them to do. It is time that the professional workers in every social service field convince the public and their leaders that the problems are known and that many of them are solvable. A great many social problems can be solved through greater cooperation among the schools, the homes, and all agencies and institutions concerned with developing the American way of life.

---

[10] *Handbook on Programs of the U.S. Department of Health, Education and Welfare*, Washington, D.C.: U.S. Government Printing Office, 1962.

WHAT IS THE SELF?

Actually, our insights and understandings with respect to the objectives of American education go beyond those described in professional statements and articles of faith. We know that at least two additional objectives are important in the education and development of the American citizen: (1) understanding of the self as a human being, and (2) the development of moral sensitivity. Too many Holden Caulfields search for identity, acceptance, and understanding without a real chance of ever finding them. There are too many persons who complete formal education programs without developing a sense of moral sensitivity and responsibility.

But what is the self? How should one search for it? Extracting and paraphrasing from the literature,[11] the writer would venture the following description: *The self is the totality of thoughts and feelings which constitutes a person's awareness of his individual existence, his conception of who and what he is.* Descartes was more correct than he realized when he said, "I think, therefore, I am." He would have been more profound had he coupled the insight of rationality with the dimension of human feelings.

The self is not given at birth — it has to be achieved. Self and personality emerge from experience in living. "Today, I remember some of my thoughts of yesterday; and tomorrow I shall remember some of my thoughts of both yesterday and today; and I am subjectively certain that they are the thoughts of the same person."[12]

Each person's self is something individual, and yet social interaction is important in its development. This fact has meaningful implications for the educator because many of the strongest social influences impinge on the child by way of his experiences at school.

The very process of living involves continuous impact between the individual and the outside world. But the internal reality for the human being is tremendously more intensive and extensive than is the contemporary external reality at any given moment. Thus, the child in school perceives, interprets, accepts, or rejects the experiences he meets at school in consideration of the self-system he manifests at the moment.

---

[11]*See:* Gordon W. Allport, *Becoming*, New Haven: Yale University Press, 1955; *Perceiving, Behaving, Becoming*, 1962 Yearbook, Washington, D.C.: Association for Supervision and Curriculum Development, 1962; Arthur T. Jersild, *In Search of Self*, New York: Bureau of Publications, Teachers College, Columbia University, 1952; Rollo May, *Man's Search for Himself*, New York: W. W. Norton & Co., 1955; Abraham H. Maslow, *Toward a Psychology of Being*, Princeton, N. J.: D. Van Nostrand Co., 1962.

[12]Allport, *op. cit.*, p. 43.

As educators, we know that the opportunities to grow and develop are directly related to the extent to which a person can give his self and his wholeness to any learning situation. While it is true that for some people learning may require labor and considerable effort, it should not — and indeed cannot — be measured by its painfulness. Learning is achieved when a person undergoes a change within himself by means of discovering his own resources and capacities. The desire to try and to grow, the force to self-realization, the quest for one's own identity — these make education possible.

Education, if it is related to the processes of life itself, can be a rather exciting experience. Many in professional education have argued this point for years. Yet the critics continue to suggest that a more rigorous education is needed, this to be achieved by pounding away and disciplining anew in order to force a new dimension of intellectual quality on the American child and adult. The problem is that this type of education may not free the mind, but may only serve to condition the person to blind acceptance of any self-constituted authority — educational, social, or political. The search for self will not be found through intellectual achievement alone. The universal language of the self is not found in the transmission of highly abstract intellectual concepts. As Arthur Jersild has noted:

> The language of thought and logical reasoning changes as people become more learned and more sophisticated. In the realm of logic, symbolic relationships become more intricate. But the language of basic human emotions does not change much. The choice of words changes, but feelings have an underlying meaning which is the same for the four-year-old and the eighty-year-old. In the domain of feeling, there is a Promethean fire which burns alike through all the ages and generations of man.

> A railroad can be a socio-economic boundary line, but emotions are not bound by it. Fear in the rich is the same as fear in the poor. Children know acceptance and rejection on both sides of the railroad track.

> It is possible for people to communicate on an emotional level even though they are poles apart in intellectual ability. The "slow learner," so dubbed by his brighter fellows, knows anger and is acquainted with grief much as his peer who has the high I.Q., and who is the darling in many present-day schools. Some of our humble slow learners may have as profound a grasp of psychological truths as their brilliant classmates.[13]

---

[13] Jersild, *op. cit.*, pp. 31–32.

The truly educated person manifests emotional maturity as well as intellectual achievement. Emotional maturity does not imply negation of emotion. Mature emotional behavior at any level of growth is that which fully reflects a healthy development of all the interacting aspects of a person's make-up. It is based on the full scope of the individual's capacities and resources and his ability to use and enjoy them.

Emotional maturity means the degree to which the person has realized his potential for richness in living, and has developed his capacity to enjoy things; to live wholeheartedly; to laugh, to feel genuine sorrow; to feel anger when faced with thwarting that would rile the temper of any sensible person; to experience fear when there is occasion to be frightened, without the false mask of courage which must be assumed by those who are so frightened that they dare not reveal to others or admit to themselves that they are afraid.[14]

The mature person has learned how to love and how to accept love. It is the giving of one's self and one's concern for other people that characterize love and make life meaningful. Even Oswald Spengler, that rather historical prophet of doom, suggested that the meaning implied in the relationships between two people who understand and "care" is perhaps as beautiful and mature an idea as any expressed by language. Spengler wrote:

The purest symbol of an understanding . . . is the old peasant couple sitting in the evening in front of their cottage and entertaining one another without a word's being passed, each knowing what the other is thinking and feeling. Words would only disturb the harmony. From such a state of reciprocal understanding something or other reaches back, far beyond the collective existence of the higher animal-world, deep in the primeval history of free-moving life.[15]

With respect to the objective of achieving moral sensitivity, or the state of being morally responsible, too many of our citizens display a condition of non-living today. Some persons have suggested that perhaps our very civilization precludes the development of moral responsibility, but this need not be so. Maslow has written a case for self-determination:

Life is a continual series of choices for the individual in

---

[14]*Ibid.*, p. 41.

[15]*The Decline of the West*, Vol. II, New York: Alfred A. Knopf Co., 1939, p. 137.

which a main determinant of choice is the person as he already is (including his goals for himself, his courage or fear, his feelings of responsibility, his ego-strength, or "will-power," etc.). We can no longer think of the person as "fully determined" where this phrase implies "determined only by forces external to the person." The person, insofar as he *is* a real person, is his own main determinant. Every person is, in part, "his own project" and makes himself.[16]

We do now find that there are people who accept a level of life much lower than that of which they are capable, and much less than either the individual or society should allow. There are too many "phony people" in the world who frustrate those persons who do seek principles of life, search for the self, and attempt to rise above the moment.

Society has never been particularly concerned with people who live innocuous lives and fail to do anything constructive. While it is true that organic malfunction and/or extreme frustration and anxiety may cause deterioration of perceptual and affective powers, it has become almost fashionable for some people to attempt escapement of the responsibility for self in relationship to the society at large.[17] Persons who blame someone else for their condition of non-living, or who fail to assume responsibility for their own actions, even their own lives, might then be called ill, mentally ill. Indeed, these people are ill, but the prognosis is only favorable when such a person is afforded the insight to realize that there are choices he can make as to how life can be lived and fulfilled. This is true of all mankind. Thus, the ultimate objective of education will be attained only when every person finds a productive capacity of self and a moral responsibility which he can share with other people.

MORE IN LIFE THAN OUT OF IT

The silent hours steal on. Educators and social workers cannot afford to remain silent. They must become more vocal, more articulate and more sophisticated in presenting not only the case for education, but for our civilization as well. Regardless of what pride we may feel in exploring the immensities of space, perhaps we would do infinitely

---

[16]A. H. Maslow, "Some Basic Propositions of a Growth and Self-Actualization Psychology," in *Perceiving, Behaving, Becoming: A New Focus for Education*, 1962 Yearbook, edited by Arthur W. Combs, Washington, D.C.: Association for Supervision and Curriculum Development, 1962, p. 36.

[17]May, *op. cit.*

more for mankind, for the welfare of humanity, for the peace and safety of the world, if we could send into the nations of the earth men and women who were truly educated as world citizens and who could dedicate their minds and lives to the service of improving the conditions of mankind.

Norman Cousins has called our age one of desensitization. Perhaps we have become desensitized to the real purposes of life and the legitimate and appropriate ways by which man is able to achieve these purposes. Cousins writes:

> The essential task, then, is to regenerate the vital responses, to reopen access to the clarifying functions of conscience, to restore the capacity to dream about a better life. Despite all the billowing evidence to the contrary, man is still capable of good purposes and decent works. He can still recapture command of his existence and the forces that are shaping it. And this regeneration requires only an experience in self-recognition to become real.[18]

As in the past, there are always two paths before us. We can conceive of life as being valuable and worth embellishment, or we can become frustrated and neurotic as did Holden Caulfield. We can practice a philosophy which suggests that life is worthwhile, that the search for self is important, that moral sensitivity and responsibility are imperative. We can acknowledge that the "becoming" of another person is highly significant, and that educators, social workers, and those who practice the healing arts have tremendous roles to play in helping other people find self-realization and the "good life."

A wise old American philosopher believed that "education is life." And the real life, whatever else it may be, is a design in symmetry, an experiment in beauty, a journey of "becoming." As educators perhaps we will have reached our goals when mankind wishes for more *in* life than out of it.

---

[18]*Saturday Review*, October 27, 1962, p. 24.

8. *Communication and the Improvement of Professional Performance*

IN A BRIEF PRESENTATION, it is difficult for one to cover such a broad topic as "communication and the improvement of professional performance." Essentially, these passing observations represent some general ideas and research findings which might motivate further study. It is hoped that a consideration of the importance of "good" communication will help in developing new insights with respect to the improvement of professional competence in any field.

Communication generally involves symbolism and, more specifically, language, whether this be a spoken dialect, a stone inscription, a telegraphic signal, or a chain of binary numbers pulsing in a modern computing machine.[1] Communication may be studied from many points of view including linguistics, mathematics, perception, or semantics. Since World War II, at least, machines have also been developed as agents of communication. Indeed the modern computing machine is indicative of man's creative effort to break certain barriers of communication which relate to his limitations of memory and speed-performance: In computational work, the machines have proved to be much faster and more accurate than the human being.[2]

Generally educators are concerned with the subject not so much as specialists of communication and its media, but as persons interested in the development of skills which enable us to learn and to teach others. At least two major subtopics relating to communication seem essential: (1) a general theory of communication, and (2) communication in action. Communication *per se* is the integral element of "good education." Improved communication will lead to a more meaningful education in any field.

Today the failure of communication is a most important factor in the misunderstanding among men of any organization or society. Lack of effective communication may be responsible for failures to achieve the goals of any organization or profession. Failure to com-

---

[1] Colin Cherry, *On Human Communication*, New York: John Wiley & Sons, Inc., 1957, p. 32.

[2] *See:* Norbert Wiener, *The Human Use of Human Beings; Cybernetics and Society*, Garden City, New York: Doubleday & Company, Inc., 1954.

municate becomes the nub of many real problems in both teaching and learning.

With respect to helping other people learn new patterns of behavior, physical or intellectual, researchers have noted repeatedly that individuals will perform successfully and even accept orders when they (1) understand what is expected, (2) believe it to be consistent with objectives of the social system, (3) think it is compatible with personal interests, and (4) find that they are mentally and physically capable of complying. The same things are true with teaching. Learning can take place, and certainly at the cognitive level, only when communication is open and free.[3]

It has been noted that good communication — free communication — with or between people is always therapeutic and educational. Psychiatrists have developed this principle. Psychiatric techniques are designed to develop communication between the specialist and persons with severe emotional handicaps. Essentially, the psychiatrist or clinical psychologist re-educates the patient by using highly developed communicative techniques. Teachers at any level of educational instruction, even those of us who deal mostly with stable personalities, could benefit from a knowledge of communication theories and techniques used by trained counselors engaged in helping other people change their perception of themselves and of the world about them.

The entire teaching process is based on man's ability to communicate. And regardless of the teaching method used in the classroom, the teacher is the primary agent of communication.

At best, communication proceeds in the face of many uncertainties. It has the character of numerous indirect inferences. Our attempt to communicate through speech may be quite difficult. Uncertainties of articulated sounds, accents and tones, uncertainties of the language itself, and uncertainties relating to the specific past experiences and the current condition of the listener all bear upon the necessity to improve communication ability if we wish to improve our teaching skills and effectiveness.

A GENERAL THEORY OF COMMUNICATION

Much is written about communication today, and many of us have been convinced of its importance in developing our professional com-

---

[3]*See:* Chester T. Barnard, *The Functions of the Executive*, Cambridge: Harvard University Press, 1938; F. Robert Paulsen, "Professors Can Improve Teaching," *Improving College and University Teaching*, Summer, 1961.

petence and achievement. It seems logical to locate an adequate general theory which becomes a model through which more effective communication might be developed.

It is the thesis of this paper that a theory of communication must take into consideration an understanding of self, of man's cosmologies, of specific barriers to communication, and of the effective use of an adequate vocabulary.

The Understanding of Self. It has become a tenet of many educational philosophies that one cannot teach or otherwise influence others until there is an understanding of self in relationship to the philosophies and cosmologies accepted as valid and real by other people.

The "self" is the totality of thoughts, feelings, and experience which constitutes a person's awareness of his individual existence, his conception of who and what he is. The self is achieved; it is not available at birth. Selfhood and personality emerge from experiences in living. Each person's self is something individual, and yet social interaction is important in self-development.[4]

There is much about the self of which we are really not aware nor certainly very articulate. Thus, a great part of the self is dispossessed. We experience communication from within and from the internal reality which is a great part of us. But that which is known only as a vague emotional feeling may be crystallized only infrequently. Much of our thinking and feeling is not verbalized, not communicated overtly in behavior. And yet all of these things are part of the self.

In a theory of communication, we must start with an intrapsychic approach. When we speak of education or the teaching-learning process, we need to ask ourselves in what way can we provide experiences which will help other individuals achieve an understanding of self as well as of other people. Ostensibly, the human task is to proceed from being ambiguous about self to a position of self-clarity and self-delineation. One of the problems, therefore, in the educational process is how to improve self-communication as it relates to helping other people achieve the capacity for self-decision and acquire new insights leading to self-fulfillment.

Communication with other individuals, and particularly those living out of their normal social group, can become extremely difficult. In many instances, the pupil in school finds himself in a new social group. This is particularly true of the young children in the first years of elementary education. The perceptions held by these pupils about

---

[4]*See:* Arthur Jersild, *In Search of Self*, New York: Bureau of Publications, Teachers College, Columbia University, 1952.

themselves become important in consideration of the teaching efforts and educational process *per se*.

In the same sense that our perceptual assumptions about other people determine how we perceive these other people to be, communication really has psychological import for any profession and particularly teaching. The other person, who is external, is always matched by our experience with him which then makes him an internal "other" person. The question becomes: Indeed, with whom are we working?

One way of approaching this problem is to ask the perennial philosophical question: What is reality anyway? For our purposes, we might say that reality is whatever it is plus our perceptual assumptions about it. This means that reality is constructed partly in the self. It is not totally perceived outside: it is fused with our assumptions about our daily and diverse experiences. In a definite work on communication, Colin Cherry has said:

> We do not perceive more than a minute fraction of the sights and sounds that fall upon our sense organs, the great majority pass us by. They make physical impressions on our retinas or in our ears, but seem not to have any effect upon our subsequent perception, thoughts, or behavior. We do not perceive and know things as they are; we perceive signs, and from these signs make inferences and build mental models of the world; we say we see and hear it; we talk about real things.[5]

It can only be concluded that much of what we think we know is only mental experience, and that the orderly world we see is not totally outside of us.

To the extent, therefore, that our perceptual assumptions are high distortions of the real other person, and in our case the students, and to the extent to which we do not actually communicate in order to correct these perceptual distortions, then we may live and work with other people for several years and not know really who they are.

People tend to distort all the time. There is an emotional push toward distortion in all of us. And a person who is physically ill or neurotic has a greater tendency to make the present nothing but the past. As teachers, we have experienced the situation wherein students cannot give of themselves and of their wholeness to the present learning situation. They find it difficult to allow themselves to change with the present circumstances. They cannot give full commitment to the present task before them. They keep a great deal of the self out of the

---

[5] Cherry, *op. cit.*, p. 260–61.

present experiences because of disinterest or anxiety. Thus, in a very real sense, the dispossessed self does not get an education, does not change behavior in ways which would be most beneficial to the individual or to the society.

Communication is the way in which we hope — if it is fluid, if it is transactional, if it gives a two-way message — to keep the internal other person conscious of himself and aware of "real" situations and relationships between himself and the universe.

Perhaps one of the troubles with professors and teachers is that, in terms of their own self-image, they have a feeling, from their own perception of themselves, that they are warm, understanding, open persons, and that they are so perceived by their students. They are disappointed when they hear "feedback," sometimes critical, indicating that the contrary is perceived to be true.

The consciousness of self, the capacity to see one's self as though from the outside, is the distinctive characteristic of man. This capacity underlies man's ability to use symbols, which is a way of disengaging something from what it is, and to develop sounds which stand for whole classes of things as well as for specific items. Man's consciousness of himself has been called the source of his highest qualities.[6] Man's consciousness of himself is related directly to his ability to communicate of himself and his perceptions of the outside world. Certainly, an understanding of self will lead to more effective communication; in conceiving of a model for improved communication, a person might consider seriously the kind of person he really is and, more importantly, the kind of person he is perceived to be by others.

Man's Cosmologies and Communication. It has been suggested that an understanding of man's cosmologies is also important in any attempt to communicate effectively with other people. All approaches to education seem to have a more or less elaborate conception of the nature of man. Nicholas Hobbs said:

> Man contantly engages in building, repairing, extending and modifying cognitive structures which help him make personal sense out of the world. The individual must have a cognitive house in which to live. This protects him from the incomprehensibilities of existence, as well as to provide some architecture for daily experiencing.[7]

---

[6] Rollo May, *Man's Search for Himself*, New York: W. W. Norton & Company, 1953, pp. 84–85.

[7] "Sources of Gain in Psychotherapy," *American Psychologist*, Vol. 17, November, 1962, p. 746–47.

The healthy man has found a purpose to life, which may not be teleological, but must at least be personal. Hobbs continues by noting that man "has to build a defense against the absurd in the human condition, and at the same time find a scheme that will make possible reasonably accurate predictions of his behavior, and of the behavior of his wife, his boss, his teacher, his physician, his neighbor, and of the policeman on the corner. He must adopt or invent a personal cosmology."[8] He invests this cosmology with faith and passion. It must be convincing to him. It must relate reasonably well to the cosmologies of other people in society, or he runs the risk of being considered sociopathic. It must serve him to the greatest extent when he becomes threatened, ill, under attack, or otherwise insecure. In times of stress or incapacitation, the ability to adjust and obtain new insights becomes more difficult. The attempt to provide new insights and concepts during periods of anxiety can have meaning only within the cosmological system perceived real to the person.

Among challenges confronting the teacher is that of providing experiences to the student which give evidence of understanding the student as a person, as a self, understanding his cosmology, if not his total philosophy. The value of any educational experience and the effectiveness of any communication will depend on the extent to which they provide an opportunity for a person to feel and perceive a closeness to another human being without fear of physical or emotional injury.

If there is a greater awareness and understanding of the self, and a greater understanding of man's philosophies, there will be improvement in communication. Logically, there should be, therefore, improvement in educational practice and achievement.

Barriers to Communication. There are many barriers to communication inherent within many subjects of study, teaching methods, or planned learning experiences. The trained and experienced teacher knows that a single idea without a well-defined meaning may distort the intent of the message or desired conceptual development of the learner. For example, there was an anthropologist who began his erudite lecture on the history of man with the statement: "When it comes to a consideration of the origin of man, let me say at the outset, everything the Bible says about the subject is false." The subject matter of the lecture was rather brilliant from this point on, but for many persons in the class, communication ended the instant the opening remark was made. The statement elicits a barrier to effective com-

---

[8]*Ibid.*

munication and teaching. The barrier becomes a fulcrum to separate opposing values.[9]

It has also been suggested that a major barrier to mutual inter-personal communication is our very natural tendency to judge, evaluate, or approve or disapprove immediately the statement of another person or another group.[10] One's primary reaction to many things spoken or written is to evaluate it from one's own frame of reference. Real communication occurs, and the evaluative tendency is avoided, when we listen with understanding. In real communication, we must be astute enough to recognize how an expressed idea or attitude is per-ceived from the other person's point of view.

Carl Rogers has written on developing greater understanding by eliminating the tendency to evaluate immediately the message we see or hear.

> It is an approach which we have found extremely potent in the field of psychotherapy. It is the most effective agent we know for altering the basic personality structure of an individual and for improving his relationships and his communications with others. If I can listen to what he can tell me, if I can understand how it seems to him, if I can see its personal meaning for him, if I can sense the emotional flavor which it has for him, then I will be releasing potent forces of change in him.[11]

Another barrier to communication is our failure to develop good listening habits. Somehow we tend to think of communication in a unilateral sense and fail to see the importance of listening in develop-ing correct patterns of effective communication. Condemning a speak-er's subject as uninteresting before analyzing its values, criticizing the speaker's delivery, preparing an answer to a point before compre-hending the point, listening only for facts, and feigning attention are all indicative of bad listening habits.[12]

Ralph Nichols and his colleagues at the University of Minnesota have called our attention to the importance of listening in the com-municative and educative process.[13] At least some studies have indi-

---

[9] Paulsen, *op. cit.*

[10] Carl L. Rogers, *Harvard Business Review*, Vol. XXX, No. 4, July-Aug-ust, 1952, pp. 46–52.

[11] *Ibid.*

[12] *See:* Ralph G. Nichols, "Listening Instruction in the Secondary School," *Bulletin*, National Association of Secondary School Principals, Vol. 36, May, 1952.

[13] *See:* Ralph G. Nichols and Leonard A. Stevens, *Are You Listening*, New York: McGraw-Hill Book Company, Inc., 1957.

cated that in consideration of reading, writing, speaking, and listening, we may perhaps spend as much as 60 to 65 per cent of our time in listening.[14] We have assumed that learning to read will automatically teach us to listen. This is not true. Many persons who study barriers to communication believe that the development of skills in listening might indeed be the most fruitful and successful avenue to improved education and certainly improved teaching.

Listening is a skill that can be taught. Some educators are beginning to recognize this fact. It is time that each teacher consider carefully how every pupil might be taught this important skill of listening. If people would learn how to analyze each topic or conversation for values of personal interest, to listen for central ideas, and to seek frequent exposition with difficult aural presentations, there would be improvement in communicative effectiveness.

Vocabulary. Another factor, at least in any theory of communication for our use, and particularly as it is related to language and the profession of education, concerns an adequate and precise vocabulary. While it is true that a professional vocabulary may become highly developed and sophisticated for the teacher and professor, it must be remembered that the objective of teaching is to help pupils and students learn and achieve. Effective communication must be considered as the coordinating activity among teachers, lay persons, and students as they seek to understand the condition in which the communicant finds himself and the results which might be expected from communicating meaning to one other.

Professional people have a responsibility to communicate current practice and research findings in acceptable ways to their own professional groups. It is assumed, however, that a professional vocabulary does not develop for itself alone, nor certainly for purposes of limiting communication to only the most sophisticated persons in the field.

It is suggested that whereas the professional vocabulary may be highly developed and specialized to indicate preciseness and validity, such a vocabulary may not be adequate for purposes of general communication. One can only suggest that effective communication for all parties and groups concerned with any professional activity must indicate more than vocabulary. Communication must include meaning as well as the formal and correct use of words or other symbols.

---

[14]*Ibid.*

COMMUNICATION IN ACTION

Communication encompasses all human behavior which results in an exchange of meaning. How well we are able to perform in our respective roles depends upon how efficiently we communicate.

Several years ago, someone drafted a statement called the "Ten Commandments of Good Communication."[15] These commandments or rules are simple, but undoubtedly have significant implications for communication in action. These commandments can be paraphrased as follows:

1. *Seek to Clarify Your Ideas Before Communication.* The more systematically one analyzes the idea or practice to be communicated, the clearer it becomes. This is the first step toward effective communication. Many communications fail because of inadequate planning. Good planning must consider the goals and attitudes, not only of the communicator, but also of those who will be affected.

2. *Examine the True Purpose of Each Communication.* Before you communicate, ask yourself what you really want to accomplish with your message. Do you want to obtain information, initiate action, change another person's attitude or behavior? Identify your most important goal, then adapt your language, tone, and total approach to serve the specific objective. Do not try to accomplish too much with each communication. The sharper the focus of your message, the greater its chances of success.

3. *Consider the Total Physical and Human Setting Wherever You Communicate.* We have noted that meaning and intent are not conveyed by words alone. Many other factors influence the overall impact of communication. One's sense of timing, the circumstances under which one communicates, the physical setting, and the immediate status of the recipient are all important factors. Thus, we must be aware constantly of the total setting. Communication, like all living things, must be capable of adapting to a specific environment.

4. *Consult with Others, Where Appropriate, in Planning Communications.* Frequently it is desirable or necessary to seek the participation of other persons in planning a communication. Consultation often helps to lend additional insight and objectivity to your message. Moreover, those who have helped plan a communication will give their active support to its message.

5. *Be Mindful, While You Communicate, of the Overtones as well as the Basic Content of Your Message.* Your tone of voice, your expression, your apparent receptiveness to the responses of others all have

---

[15] Author unknown.

tremendous impact on those you wish to reach. These subleties often affect a listener's reaction to a message even more than its basic content. Similarly, your choice of language — particularly your awareness of the fine shades of meaning and emotion in the words you use — predetermines in large part the reactions of your listeners.

6. *Take the Opportunity, When it Arises, to Convey Something of Help or Value to the Receiver.* Consideration of the other person's interest and needs, the habit of trying to look at things from his point of view, will frequently point up opportunities to convey something of immediate benefit or long-range value to the listener. Remember the barriers to effective communication, and attempt to develop communication along lines which are perceived to be of value to the other person as well as to yourself.

7. *Follow Up Your Communication.* Our vast efforts at communication may be wasted, and we may never know whether we have succeeded in expressing our true meaning and intent, if we do not follow up to see how well our message has been received. Make certain that every important communication has a "feedback" so that complete understanding and appropriate action result.

8. *Communicate for Tomorrow as well as for Today.* While communications may be aimed primarily at meeting the demands of an immediate situation, they must be planned with the past in mind if they are to appear consistent with the receivers' frames of reference. Most important of all, communication must be consistent with long-range interests and goals. It is not always easy to report a poor prognosis or a critical appraisal relating to the listener. But postponing disagreeable communications makes them more difficult in the long run and is actually unfair to all parties concerned.

9. *Be Sure Your Actions Support Your Communication.* In the final analysis, the most important persuasive kind of communication is not what you say but what you do. When a man's actions or attitudes contradict his words, we tend to discount what he has said. For every professional person, the meaning is that professionalism is more an attitude of mind and ultimate performance than it is an evidence of degrees and diplomas hanging on the office wall.

10. *Last, but by No Means Least: Seek not only to be Understood, but to Understand — Be a Good Listener.* When we start talking, we often cease to listen. Listening is one of the most important, most difficult, and most neglected skills in communication. It demands that we concentrate not only on the explicit meanings another person is expressing, but on the implicit meanings as well. The unspoken thoughts and overtones may be far more significant than the spoken word. Thus, we must not only learn to listen for this articulate mes-

sage, but must also learn to listen with the inner ear if we are to know the inner man.

CONCLUSIONS

Meaningful messages are available from all kinds of signs impinging on the daily life of every person. Communication in all of its aspects obviously covers an enormous field. Communication by language, however, is one of man's distinctive abilities. The teacher and professor should be aware that although language is a primary means human beings use in discovering reality, there are other forms of communication also important in helping other people learn.

The study of communication proceeds as a subject of inquiry in various scientific fields. Communication is being studied through the development of machines which speak to one another through a specific language. Communication is being studied by means of specific programs involving controlled and experimental groups of people. And, communication is being studied through the observations which become the principal data of the clinical sciences.

There is little doubt that the need to improve communication is a burning problem in the society today. In a society which struggles with casualness, impersonality, and anonymity, there is an imperative to learn to communicate more effectively with one another.

In the last analysis, one's education is influenced to a great extent by the teacher who is a master of the language. Teachers who insist that students read the great literature, listen to the wellspoken word, and learn to write and speak effectively are helping these students build a solid educational foundation. Teachers must know that direct communication between minds is impossible, not only physically but psychologically. Communication can be achieved only in a roundabout way. Thought must pass first through meanings, and then through words. Teachers must be concerned with words, but must always be aware of thoughts and meanings.

It is said that a word is a microcosm of human consciousness. Language is the cosmic force which promotes the very concept of humanity. In many ways, the master teacher is the master of language. Such a teacher will surely motivate students to thought and in turn help them transfer thought to expression. It is in the development of expression that the man emerges from the child and human competence is achieved. Human competence is the primary goal of all education.

9. Transcending Our Heritage

HUMAN LIFE HAS ALWAYS APPEARED CHEAP in some parts of the world. Really, life is not cheap in any country, but as we have heard and read about the historical problems of famine, war, and disease in the nations of the Far East, we have concluded that the lives of many human beings scarcely suggest the birthright or might achieve the significance which we consider possible and desirable in the nations of the West. To know about the ways and conditions of mankind is not enough today, however, and thus educators must assume more responsibility for teaching about the commonalities of humankind. There is need today for every person to have a greater understanding about man and his many cultures. There is an imperative need to develop appreciative attitudes among all men concerning what it means to be human. There is need to manifest actual reverence for life. There is a need to work toward building a world wherein peace and not war is the common condition.

Respecting the need of understanding man and his diverse cultures, the following story may be somewhat illustrative:

During World War II, a group of American soldiers stood on the bank of a river in an Orient land. At the time, a funeral procession for a young Chinese boy passed down the roadway. Four men carried a crude casket-type box containing the body. The mourners followed, and it was evident that sorrow filled the hearts of family and friends. Some of these people wore strange-looking robes, and some carried paraphernalia seemingly of poor quality. While the other traditions we associate with funerals probably took place, this procession had one unusual feature. It was led by a brass band playing a dissonant selection — on the theme of "Three Blind Mice."

The sight and the sound of this funeral procession seemed more than strange to the foreign soldiers in that land. They thought: "What funny people to have a band playing 'Three Blind Mice' at a funeral!"

And yet as one reflects on that experience, many questions and possible answers are noted. Perhaps the Chinese family was trying to adopt a supposed cultural trait of Western civilization, that of providing a special musical tribute at a funeral. Perhaps a trained anthropologist might have recognized an element of cultural diffusion. Perhaps the entire incident could only be interpreted in the most simple ways relating to the impoverished circumstances of many people living in this locality.

There is little need to speculate on an anthropological interpretation. It is sufficient to note that those in the funeral party were probably quite oblivious to the reaction of strangers who perceived the incident as unsophisticated, if not amusing. But the fact that the perception of one group of human beings was devoid of depth and understanding of the feelings and circumstances of another group of human beings is of concern to those of us interested in education. It can certainly be concluded that both groups were really "foreign" to each other.

As these men witnessed the funeral procession at the Chinese cemetery, surely the one truth which should have been noted was not that the band played an unusual selection or that the people were poorly dressed. Rather, it should have been noted that the grief of a mother for a lost son in one country of the world could be as great as that of a mother confronted with the same loss in any other country — as great even as in our own land. The similarity and equality of emotional response really suggest the concept of "brotherhood of man." In many ways, it could have been noted that while history may indicate that life is cheap in some areas of the world, the thinking and feeling human being everywhere has recognized the importance of every person. Essentially, the lack of natural resources, inadequate education, and the general fact of historical severity are most responsible for the idea that the human being is considered less important in some countries than in others.

THE NEED FOR EDUCATION

Inadequate education is the real barrier to understanding foreign peoples of various cultures in general. Indeed, a lack of understanding about the nature and potentiality of man and a lack of concern for one's neighbor remain two of the basic problems confronting the entire world. To help develop a greater understanding among men and to help people develop the capacity to "care" and to be concerned about others are important objectives of modern education. Insofar as human progress is concerned, the teaching of facts may become rather sterile unless these facts are related to ways and means by which the human race might be improved.

It has been said that "education is a search for truth." It has also been noted that truth is like a great road — it is really not difficult to find. The great evil of life may be only that men sometimes fail to seek it. If horizons are expanded, and if men really care, many additional truths remain to be found.

Education has been called the acquisition of the cultural posessions of the race with a view toward achieving one's own potentiality in relationship to the betterment of society. In many ways, these cultural possessions have been called "spiritual," and include knowledge and understanding of the great institutional, literary, scientific, and religious achievements of mankind.[1] And in America today, we have developed school systems and educational institutions surpassed by none other in the history of the world to help boys, girls, men, and women achieve an education and find both personal and societal fulfillment.

THE BASIC ASSUMPTION OF EDUCATION

What is the basic assumption of education? How important is education in the development of our great civilizations? What are the great objectives of education in America today?

Perhaps you will recall the story of Ulysses, that Greek hero of old. Ulysses sailed the known seas of his day and visited many of the strange and foreign lands. The story of Ulysses and the Sirens, as told by the Greek poet Homer in the *Odyssey*, holds considerable interest for those engaged in education.

On this voyage from Troy, Ulysses and his crew had to pass the Island of the Sirens. The Sirens were mythical creatures who lured sailors to destruction on the rocks around their island. They sang an apparently irresistible song — a song so attractive that seafaring men were willing to gamble with their lives in the attempt to hear what the Sirens had to say.

Ulysses was determined to hear what they sang. Thus he had his men tie him to the mast, while they, with ears plugged with wax, rowed the ship past the reefs. What did the Sirens say? Homer tells us. They made no appeal to Ulysses' physical senses, but rather they said: "Come hither, glorious Ulysses, and go your way the wiser.... For we know all things, all that hath been, and all that shall be hereafter." They appealed to man's *desire for knowledge*. They knew that for the thinking and curious man, the quest for knowledge has the strongest possible appeal.

---

[1] Nicholas Murray Butler, former President of Columbia University, defined education as "an acquisition of the spiritual possessions of the race." He developed this concept to include many of the areas listed above.

The basic assumption of education is observed in the proposition that *it is better to know than not to know.*[2] An examination of the history of mankind gives evidence of the fact that man's desire to know and to learn has been the greatest motivating factor in all of his accomplishments. In many ways, man's desire to know has been equated to his attempt to become a "free person." Even the scriptures have magnified this concept by suggesting that in knowing the truth, man would be free.

But to say that "knowledge is power" becomes a platitude at times. We need to review this statement occasionally. Knowledge gives us the power to control ourselves and the affairs of our life. It affords us the prospects of living without fear, thinking through our problems, and making wise decisions as we attempt to fulfill our ambitions and reach our personal objectives. Knowledge provides us the key to understanding and an appreciation of our own life and the lives of our fellow men.

But education is of little value if it leads only to knowledge or contemplation. The real objectives of education must go beyond knowledge held for its sake alone. Knowledge must be equated to behavior, and education must be evaluated in terms of both what is known and what is used.

EDUCATION — IDEALS AND YOUTH

Intelligent action and behavior should, and most generally will, operate on and through principles. Sometimes we list ideals and then call them principles. In America, we proclaim many of them as symbolic of our way of life. We find them listed with different words, but always the same meanings. The following ten items have been called the tenets of our American philosophy.

1. The dignity of man and the value of the human personality
2. The moral responsibility of every individual
3. Institutions as the servants of man
4. The principle of common consent
5. Our desire for and devotion to truth
6. Our respect for excellence in every endeavor
7. Our belief in moral equality
8. Our belief in the brotherhood of man

---

[2]*See:* Charles J. Armstrong, "The Role of the Teacher," *Improving College and University Teaching*, Winter, 1957.

9. Our individual right to the pursuit of happiness
10. Spiritual enrichment through freedom of worship

But education toward or acceptance of these principles does not start with formal schooling in the first grade and stop at graduation from high school or college. Education has been called life itself. As one author has suggested:

> Education . . . begins with a mother's look, with a father's nod of approbation, or a sign of reproof; with a sister's gentle pressure of the hand, or a brother's noble act of forbearance: with handfuls of feathers in green dells, on hills, and daisy meadows, with bird's nests admired, but not touched; with creeping ants, and almost imperceptible emmets; with humming bees and glass beehives, with pleasant walks in shady lanes, and with thoughts directed in sweet and kindly tones and words to nature, to beauty, to acts of benevolence, to virtue, and to the source of all good, to God himself.[3]

The end of education must always remain the possibility of continuous development of self in relationship to fellow man and society at large. And one's development and success must be substantiated in personal behavior, purposeful action, and a manifestation of productivity for the welfare of all humanity.

Mary Wilson Ross has stated a limitation and constant problem confronting us:

> No matter if man should be able to at least establish a bridgehead on the pitted surface of the moon. Or if he should find possible living conditions beneath the lowering clouds of the planet Venus. Or even if he perfects a rocket that would take a band of space pioneers — prepared to produce children and grandchildren en route — far beyond our Earth into another Solar system. These intrepid voyagers into space would still carry with them the very same human equipment as those they left behind. So when man conquers space, his ancient universal and perpetual problem will remain the same — as it has from the very beginning — to conquer himself.[4]

Hundreds of years after Homer wrote the *Odyssey* and told of the adventures of the Greek hero, a famous English poet also noted the significance of education as it related to the *modus vivendi* of that mythical character. In Alfred Lord Tennyson's epic poem, *Ulysses*, we note

---

[3] Author unknown.

[4] Published source unknown.

the challenge of the educational pursuit. Ulysses, the almost Faustian character of his day, an old, grey, and wise man, is heard to remark:

> For always roaming with a hungry heart
> Much I have seen and known — cities of men
> And manners, climates, councils, governments,
> Myself not least, but honoured of them all —
> And drunk delight of battle with my peers,
> Far on the ringing plains of windy Troy.
>
> I am part of all that I have met;
> Yet all experience is an arch wherethrough
> Gleams that untraveled world whose margin fades
> Forever and forever when I move.
>
> How dull it is to pause, to make an end,
> To rust unburnished, not to shine in use;
> As though to breathe were life! Life piled on life
> Were all too little, and of one to me,
> Little remains; but every hour is saved
> From the eternal silence, something more,
> A bringer of new things; and vile it were
> For some three suns to store and hoard myself,
> And this grey spirit yearning in desire
> To follow knowledge like a sinking star
> Beyond the utmost bounds of human thought.[5]

In John Gardner's book on excellence, he suggested that older people know something that their younger friends do not know — something that can never be fully understood nor communicated without having the experience brought about by age.[6] "No matter how firm an intellectual grasp the young person may have on the idea that education is a life-long process, he can never know it with the poignancy, with the deeply etched clarity, with the overtones of satisfaction and regret that an older person knows it. The young person has not yet made enough mistakes that cannot be repaired. He has not yet passed enough forks in the road that cannot be retraced."[7]

---

[5]*Immortal Poems of the English Language*, New York: Washington Square Press, 1952, p. 376.

[6]*Excellence*, New York: Harper & Brothers, 1962.

[7]*Ibid.*, p. 139.

On a large office building in Sacramento, the state capitol of California, is a sentence engraved in stone. It reads: "Give Me Men to Match My Mountains." In America, we can gaze in appreciation at the great mountains — the Rockies, the Uintas, and the Appalachians. We can traverse our great expansive plains, cross our deep, flowing rivers, travel up and down our beautiful coastal areas, and feel secure in the green wooded hills of Connecticut or Michigan. We know there is an historical challenge implied in that statement: "Give Me Men to Match My Mountains." We know that this country has produced men and women who have and do indeed match the grandeur of their native scenery. We know that the youth of today can build upon a heritage forged in honor and founded on a devotion which parents and teachers have afforded them. This devotion and affection will prove much stronger ultimately than the appeal of any philosophy which calls for the sacrifice of basic human values proved constant over the generations past. We have faith that the youth of today will give us the leadership needed tomorrow.

It is an appropriate time to reflect upon educational achievement, and upon the challenges which will confront us in the future. We must consider seriously the values of education and the responsibilities inherent in its attainment. Out of the many dates, names, pages, and books, the student need only save and remember the most significant through the passing of time. But if the future of America and of the world itself is to remain secure, the challenges to education must be met. Above all else, the men and women of tomorrow must not only understand the history of mankind and the current problems which confront the world societies, but they must also understand more fully the capabilities of each human being and the prospects of transcending the heritage into which each person is born.

10. The Challenges of Change, Conviction, and Commitment

PUBLIC EDUCATION IS OF WIDE CONCERN in America today. It is agreed generally that an educated citizenry is essential if the American system and way of life is to be maintained and developed. The specific objectives of education have been debated frequently, but it is now generally accepted that each child should be given equal educational opportunity.

When one reflects on the history of this country, he cannot remain oblivious to the contributions made by Horace Mann, Henry Barnard, and other educational pioneers. These men will always be honored not only for foresight and vision, but for conviction and commitment to the task of educating the common man in schools common to all. In cooperation with early American political leaders, these educators built the foundation upon which our national values have been developed. The public school is more than a value unto itself. The American school has become the institution wherein each child born in this nation might learn about the opportunities available for self-fulfillment and success.

We know that organized education may or may not serve the cause of human progress. At times, education has been used to propagandize specific national ideologies or philosophies of life. The very word education elicits different definitions and connotations among those people who are concerned about it. Certainly the teaching profession has not always assumed responsibility for charting the direction of the educational enterprise. An analysis of local and state community structure would show that the adult-dominant-status groups have seldom included educators within their number. In many cases, educational policy has been made by those who know least about education and the school as an important social institution. Today it is imperative that educators at least share in planning those educational programs in which they will be involved.

Essentially, it is agreed that American public education has responsibilities to (1) transmit the cultural heritage, (2) provide experiences for the development of new knowledge and new social patterns, and (3) provide situations to stimulate the creative abilities of man. Some persons have suggested that the function of formal education must become even less concerned with the inculcation of our established traditions.[1] We must now move in the direction of finding the new knowledge and skills needed in the new emerging social order. Certainly the school must not be perceived as an institution interested only in maintaining the *status quo*. The school should be the one agency in every community most concerned with changes emerging in all aspects of life.

There are compelling forces at work in the American society today. There is the complexity of the world brought about by the scientific and technological revolution of the past decades. There is more to learn and there are more pupils to be educated. People must be educated to higher levels of skills and understandings. The creative talents of mankind must be released, encouraged, and developed. It is now clearly understood that education must permeate all phases and ages of life.

From the humble beginnings of an educational system manifested by the Massachusetts Laws of 1642 and 1647, we have developed an organizational structure and diversified curricula never before seen in the annals of mankind. From a school system enrolling at most a few hundred pupils in each state, we now enroll millions of pupils in thousands of schools across the nation. In a nation and world wherein the completion of a formal education was afforded historically to a small number of the aristocracy, we have developed programs providing opportunities for nearly everyone who indicates capacity and interest.

In our concern with the pursuit of excellence in living, we must be concerned with the prospects for achieving excellence in education. Education is the key to whatever the future holds for this culture, this civilization, and the world. The teacher is the key to the development of education. We would agree with Max Lerner that "by instilling a love of books, a hunger for experience, a critical attitude toward the prevailing idols of the tribe, a generous one toward foreign peoples and alien cultures," teachers "unlock for each the treasures of history and science, literature and the arts," and place in the hands of each generation "that key to whatever has been felt and created which makes educational systems potentially revolutionary and every good teacher by necessity an insurgent."[2]

---

[1] *See:* Margaret Mead, editor, *Cultural Patterns and Technical Change*, New York: New American Library of World Literature, 1955.

[2] *America as a Civilization*, New York: Simon and Schuster, 1957, p. 738.

THE SKILLS OF TEACHING

The focus of teaching and the efforts of much research in education have been directed toward the determination of what might be considered principles of instruction. It has always seemed to me that any argument was specious if it suggested that the classroom teacher was not concerned with substantive knowledge as well as method and technique. Methods of teaching are barren if unrelated to the substance of knowledge. Thus we assume that the teacher of today possesses a substantial general education and considerable information in a major field of specialization, and in addition has learned certain skills which will help in teaching children and youth those things deemed most important by this society.

The skills of teaching follow a type of hierarchy noted in other professions. Technical, human, and conceptual skills are all required in successful practice. Briefly, let me review these three types of skills.

Technical skills are those suggesting an "understanding and proficiency in a specific kind of activity, particularly one involving methods, processes, procedures, or techniques. These skills involve specialized knowledge, analytical ability within that speciality, and facility in the use of the tools and techniques of the specific discipline."[3] The beginning classroom teacher should have acquired a significant number of technical skills.

Human skills are factors of personality which enable us to work effectively as a member of a group or to be productive in the cooperative efforts of a team. Further, human skills imply an understanding of people *qua* people, and in most instances an understanding of one's self to the extent that one might also understand another person or persons in a meaningful and productive relationship. Human skills are not easily learned by some people and are not of concern to others. Our research has indicated, however, that the most successful and influential teachers are those who have developed these skills of human relations to a point where they are accepted as both teachers and community leaders for more reasons than either superior knowledge or the status position *per se*.[4] Teachers will find that if they develop skills in human relations they will become more effective agents of change, and thus succeed in one of the major tasks demanded of educators today.

---

[3]*See:* Robert L. Katz, "Skills of an Effective Administrator," *Harvard Business Review*, Vol. 33, No. 1, January-February, 1955.

[4]*See:* Ernest R. Hilgard, "The Human Dimension in Teaching," *A.H.E. College and University Bulletin*, Vol. 17, No. 11, March 15, 1965.

Conceptual skills are said to include the ability to visualize the enterprise as a whole. Such competency indicates recognition of the various parts and functions of the organization. It has been suggested that only administrative leaders need develop these conceptual skills. I would submit, however, that every teacher is a leader, and that both teaching and learning will be facilitated in direct proportion to the overall perceptions held about educational objectives and the means needed to achieve them.

It is difficult to teach skills of a conceptual nature, and it is doubtful if our teacher-education programs at the university level are very successful in affording experience in this area to prospective teachers. In effect, we might say that we can train for technical skills; we hope to educate for human skills; and through simulated and actual experience, we might develop conceptual skills.

Classroom teachers have a responsibility to be concerned with all types of skills relating to the improvement of professional performance. And most of all, teachers should become aware that the way in which they conceptualize the total educational program is important to the ultimate success of the profession at large.

THE NEED TO IMPROVE COMMUNICATION

Permeating the art of teaching is the subject of communication. Effective communication is needed in any attempt of the teacher to transfer the knowledge he possesses or to organize educational experiences wherein students learn through self-discovery.

In recent months, much has been written about communication and the improvement of professional performance.[5] Communication must be studied as a two-way process. Too often we have been concerned only with the ability of the communicator to speak effectively or to transfer meaning through the written word. We have been most concerned with the extent and technical aspects of communication, and have to a large degree neglected the need to improve our listening ability. We should also be aware of other forms of language which may be "muted" or at best emotional. Gardner Murphy has said:

> If communication theory is conceived of only in terms of bits of verbal information received, it can miss its most fundamental role; for the world of blushing, blanching, sighing, hint-

---

[5] *See:* F. Robert Paulsen, "Communication in the Improvement of Professional Performance," *Journal of the American Physical Therapy Association,* September, 1963.

ing, and averting the eyes leads into a rich communication world that *can* be treated as communication, and which we can teach our recorders, our magnetic tapes, and our computers to understand and to use. We need to understand the whole communication process, so that such body language — or paralanguage, or semantic exchange of feeling and impulse as well as idea — will come before the multidimensional registration system of the student of man. The inner structure of man will then be seen more fully in its relation both to the social environment which he encounters and the social environment which he is forever creating.[6]

Teachers must be aware that communication is the basic component of successful practice. If teachers are not succeeding in accomplishing those objectives deemed important and desirable, it is necessary to evaluate methods of communication and perhaps to develop some workable theory for improving communicative skills. It has always seemed to me that our communication might be improved if we take into account (1) an understanding of self, (2) an understanding of various philosophies of mankind, (3) specific barriers to communication, and (4) the effective use of an adequate vocabulary. We will not elaborate on these four factors now, but our conscious effort to improve communication within the classroom will result in improved professional performance across the nation.

CHALLENGES CONFRONT US

What can one say about the challenge of change? The goal, basically, of all education is change — human change — in directions we consider appropriate. Ordinarily, when we think of the challenge of change, we dwell upon the development of the new technology in our society. Generally, however, the most prominent characteristic today is change. In view of a changing world, it is imperative that educators concern themselves with creative thinking, imagination, adaptability, and the development of sound judgment. In addition to knowledge and skills, these additional aptitudes are needed to solve the myriad problems emanating from the development of the complex society. James Reston has said:

Change is the biggest story in the world today, and we are not covering it adequately; change in the size and movement of

---

[6] "Communication and Mental Health," *Psychiatry*, Vol. 27, No. 2, 1964, p. 101.

our people, change in the nature, location, availability of jobs; violent change in the cities, and on the land; change in the relations between village and town, town and city, city and state, state and nation, and, of course, change in the relations between the empires.[7]

Our confrontation with increased knowledge in every field affords us a challenge of paramount significance. It is predicted that in the next fifteen years, scientists will learn as much more about the universe as in all previous history. In special fields, scientists agree that twice as much is known now as was known in 1950, and four times as much as in 1935.[8]

Most of us in the educational profession are concerned with current issues and changes forthcoming in the decades ahead. Recent federal legislation, and particularly the *Elementary and Secondary Education Act of 1965*, will have a profound impact on our educational system. But even without the passage of this federal legislation, it would be necessary for the local schools and individual teachers to consider ways to re-orient and improve educational objectives and practices. The schools are caught up in the technological and societal revolutions. They must respond accordingly regardless of the level of governmental support.

The following are among the educational changes and/or trends which might be anticipated during the decade ahead:

1. In the attempt to meet the challenge of quantity and quality in American public education, there will be concerted efforts to find more able teachers, to develop many diverse instructional methods, and to change the organizational patterns of our traditional schools and local districts.

2. For ten years, educators have talked about "individual differences" as if knowledge of their existence should improve the instructional techniques of teachers and the achievement of the children. The fact is well known; it is the practice which has been deficient. For the most part, we continue to teach as if all children were alike. During the next fifty years, there will be considerable emphasis on educational practices designed to help children achieve self-esteem and success by exercising and developing whatever talents and abilities are possessed by each individual. Teaching machines, self-pacing instruc-

---

[7]*See:* "The Biggest Story in the World," *The New Republic*, May 4, 1963, p. 15; Roger L. Shinn, *Tangled World*, New York: Charles Scribner's Sons, 1965.

[8]*See:* Solomon Diamond, *The World of Probability*, New York: Basic Books, Inc., 1964.

tional materials, and other educational innovations must be considered primarily as instruments wherein we might actually treat individual differences rather than philosophize about them.

3. The size and scope of the educational enterprise throughout the nation will be enlarged. During the past year, at least 50,000,000 children and adults were engaged in some formal educational activity within approximately 125,000 schools and over 2,000 colleges and universities. This enrollment represents 30 per cent of the population. There is every reason to believe that enrollments in various educational programs will increase. In addition to expanded programs and enrollments in elementary and secondary schools and in colleges and universities, there will be expanded opportunities made available in new vocational schools and technical institutes. For those young people finishing educational programs and seeking to enter the labor market, the acquiring of technical competence will be an important consideration. The overall objective of human competence will remain, however, the most important educational goal.

4. In addition to aptitudes determined, knowledge learned, and skills developed, the child and youth of today will form the basic attitudes toward life during the increased number of years spent in school. In view of the explosion of knowledge, educators must become more and more discriminating in determining what should be taught in the formal school setting. Educators must exercise more wisdom than ever before in determining those policies and practices which will exert a powerful influence on the generations to follow.

5. Science and technology will continue making a revolutionary impact upon educational programs and curricula. In a sense, schools have been isolated from technological advancement for a half-century, and the vacuum created is being rapidly filled. Scientists will indicate more interest and concern about education at all levels. Indeed, as these scientists become more involved in the development of curricula, it will be difficult to contain them in the area of substance. They will become fascinated with method and will note the similarity between some methods of instruction used by teachers and the logical-analytical approach of their own fields.

6. During the years ahead, the new techniques of storing, processing, and disseminating information will cease to be the property of a few scientists and will become accessible to all persons engaged in research and educational activities. Information retrieval systems will be developed throughout the country. Console installations connected to automated libraries and repositories will allow educators the opportunity of obtaining, almost immediately, the newest information as well as historical data on any subject. In future years, the utilization of computers, retrieval systems, and other forms of informa-

tion technology will be a part of the standard practice required of master teachers.

7. The development of mass communication and transportation, binding the world together more tightly each year, will afford considerable general information and knowledge to all citizens. Students will take to the classroom significant information about many aspects of life. Thus, teachers must become extremely knowledgeable and sophisticated about the universe as well as about their specialty.

8. In our efforts to evaluate educational programs and to determine individual student progress, various kinds of basic education tests and other intellectual achievement instruments have been developed and used. During the years ahead, measurement and evaluation programs will expand to include significant testing of attitudes, interests, values, self-understanding, potential creativeness, and the individual differences manifested in solving personal and social problems.

9. The increased amount of leisure time made available to everyone will create problems wherein educators must consider the moral and ethical issues of our society. We must recognize that neither science nor technique, neither political constitution nor majority vote will solve some of the problems confronting mankind. The teaching of values will receive considerably more emphasis in the public schools. The control we have achieved over the physical world has created severe threats to our sense of security and personal worth. Ethical conduct, therefore, becomes related to survival value, and educators must assume responsibility for promoting a new interest in this subject. Educators will be charged, more and more, with the responsibility of defining the "good life," and of helping people develop a desire to live at full capacity and potential.

10. Educators will become active instruments of social welfare and social change. There will be an increased emphasis on research. This research in educational theory and practice will indicate that cultural progress can be accomplished through more effective programs in the schools. In the years ahead, the educated man will be the man of power. The man of power will have the ability to plan, suggest, and direct the course of human events in a world demanding competence and understanding.

11. Teacher organizations in the future will play a more significant role in determining both conditions of employment for teaching personnel and the educational facilities needed for the children. Whether these organizations will remain closely associated with the concept of "profession," or whether they will develop into something akin to labor unions is difficult to determine. There is need, however, to re-evaluate the roles and relationships which exist among teachers, administrators, and members of boards of education or school com-

mittees. It seems most appropriate to seek clarification of these positional roles and functions. Either the school administrator or elected teacher representatives should maintain direct communication with the board of education concerning the needs, welfare, and aspirations of the teachers. Teachers' organizations are emerging as powerful policy groups on the educational scene. They will have considerable impact on the development of education during the years to come.

12. International education programs will continue to develop and expand. Greater emphasis will be placed on language instruction, and in the future, students in American schools will learn several languages as do their counterparts in many foreign lands today. If the ideal of "world civilization" is not appealing nor practical, the continual exchange of students to and from every nation of the world will indicate the prospects of a world at peace based on an acceptance of the dignity of the human being, the practice of human rights, and an appreciation of the many significant contributions each culture might offer mankind.

Let me suggest again, however, that basically change is brought about by the explosion of knowledge, our ability to assimilate and transmit this knowledge, and our success in effecting change for improved performance of the individual. The knowledge and routine of a previous day will scarcely be adequate for the professional services required tomorrow. The unskilled worker is obsolete in factory and farm. Society has moved to a higher economic plane and a higher standard of living. Teachers must remain motivated always to seek new knowledge and to use it in raising the level of human competence.

In-service education programs must be developed and sponsored by local school districts and organizations of classroom teachers as well as by institutions of higher learning. These kinds of programs are as essential to the profession as are those at the pre-service level. Clearly, one of the major responsibilities of educational leaders is to convince lay leaders in every community, as well as colleagues, that education is a never ending process, and that positive acceptance of change is a challenge and an opportunity to work for human welfare under the prospects of limitless possibilities. Is there any greater challenge than this?

The challenge of conviction becomes a handmaiden to the challenge of change. Change alone may create frustration, but coupled with the conviction of our assignments, we are able to maintain the security needed for ourselves individually and for the society.

The great men of history have been personalities with strong convictions. But we meet people every day who confront the challenge of conviction in ways which would have made Socrates proud. The teaching corps is not without membership indicating a conviction that the best education must be provided to all pupils who enter the classroom. The educational profession will always welcome new members who possess this conviction.

And what is conviction without commitment? The challenge of commitment becomes the most important of all. Commitment gives direction to our lives. Commitment demands choice of values and the selection of appropriate pathways leading toward human life as it ought to be. Many dedicated teachers recognize this fact, but the dedicated teacher must be committed to goals other than societal platitudes. In addition to whatever commitment is held for improving one's own profession, the effective teacher will be one who makes commitment to the task of changing society through the transformation of mankind.

> Man is a creature and creator of history because of his unique capacity to undergo transformation, psychological, social, cultural, and historical, by the sharing, the accumulation, the integration, and the expanding of all the dimensions of meaning. . . .
> Human history has scarcely yet begun. Man is yet to be created in the fullness of his being. No other form of life, as far as we know, has ever been the carrier of this creativity of history. Surely, this is a destiny immeasurably beyond any other in its grandeur and tragedy of what has happened and in the glory of its possibilities.[9]

With ultimate commitment and action, each individual finds it possible to make his mark upon the progress of mankind.

It may be commonplace to say that the education profession stands at the crossroads. And yet many educators firmly believe that this is true. We are confronted with a decision to make. We may decide to rest on the laurels of an historically proud and dedicated profession. Certainly our service and indeed our image are still lighted by the lanterns of the past as well as by the accomplishments of the present day. We may, however, accept actively the challenges of change, conviction, and commitment. We can help create not only a new education for the future, but a new society as well. Our efforts must be illuminated by the wise use of all human and technical resources made available to us. Our professional insight toward edu-

---

[9] Henry Nelson Wieman, *Man's Ultimate Commitment*, Carbondale: Southern Illinois University Press, 1963.

cational possibilities must transcend historical accomplishment and present-day dedication.

In conclusion, we must reflect again on the dedication, conviction, and commitment of Horace Mann. Trained as a lawyer, afforded countless professional and business opportunities, Horace Mann chose instead the difficult challenge of initiating, developing, and perfecting a concept of universal public education which remains as a monument to his being. Mann's foresight and faith in free American public education is noted in several of his *Common School Journals* and *Annual Reports*. Many of his statements now appear prophetic.

> Men wait until the tide of evil rises and desolates the land again and again, before they will erect barriers against the deluge. Men will not hear the wind; they wait for the whirlwind. Men will not take warning from the cloud, they wait for the tempest. And the calamities which spring from ignorance, and a neglect of the social conditions of the masses of people are no exception to this rule. Republics, one after another, — a splendid yet mournful train, — have emerged into being; they have risen to greatness, and surrounding nations have sought protection beneath the shelter of their power; but they have perished through a want of intelligence and virtue in the masses of the people.[10]

We remember his call to action:

> Collect whatever of talent, or erudition, or eloquence, or authority this broad land can supply, and go forth and teach this people.[11]

And, after a lifetime of service, Horace Mann's last address at Antioch still inspires us:

> When I think, after the experience of one life, — what I could do and would do . . . more and better than I have ever done for the cause of humanity, of temperance, of peace; for breaking the rod of the oppressor; for the higher education of the world and especially for the higher education of the best part of it — women: when I think of these things I feel the Phoenixspirit glowing within me. . . . I yearn for another warfare in behalf of the right. . . . I would enlist for another fifty years campaign, and fight it out for the glory of God and the welfare of man.[12]

---

[10]*Eighth Annual Report*, Covering the Year 1844, Boston: Dutton and Wentworth State Printers, 1845, pp. 135–36.

[11]*See:* Louise Hall Tharp, *Until Victory*, Boston: Little, Brown and Co., 1953.

[12]*Ibid.*, p. 310.

Those of us in the classroom today have been given a real opportunity to bring the idea and prospects of the "good life" to those whom we teach. The revolution in our schools has begun; teachers must carry it forward. The challenges of change, conviction, and commitment transcend the obvious concern of making quality education available to the nation's children. Education must provide solutions to those perplexing problems which confront society at large. Certainly those conditions of ignorance, superstition, disease, and poverty, and the political and economic inequities which still exist might be abolished through more adequate education. In the development of human competence and power to accomplish these objectives, the American teacher must be dedicated and committed.

One of America's foremost authors, William Faulkner, sounded a note of humility when he accepted his Nobel Prize for literature. His words and sentiment epitomize the feeling of all those persons who, in working within the educational enterprise today, confront the challenges of which we have been speaking.

> Not for glory, and least of all, not for profit, but to create something out of the human spirit, something which did not exist before.

Index